Homeward Bound

Homeward Bound

The Joy of Nature and My Life Outdoors

HAMZA YASSIN

First published in Great Britain in 2025 by Gaia,
an imprint of Octopus Publishing Group Ltd
Carmelite House
50 Victoria Embankment
London EC4Y 0DZ
www.octopusbooks.co.uk

An Hachette UK Company
www.hachette.co.uk

The authorized representative in the EEA is Hachette Ireland, 8 Castlecourt Centre,
Dublin 15, D15 XTP3, Ireland (email: info@hbgi.ie)

ISBN: 978-1-85675-541-2
eISBN: 978-1-85675-542-9

A CIP catalogue record for this book is available from the British Library.

Typeset in 13/20pt Plantin MT Pro by Six Red Marbles UK, Thetford, Norfolk.

Printed and bound in Great Britain.

3 5 7 9 10 8 6 4

Commissioning Editor: Jessica Minocha
Creative Director: Mel Four
Senior Editor: Leanne Bryan
Copy Editor: Sam Wells
Production Controller: Sarah Parry

This FSC® label means that materials used for the product have been responsibly sourced.

Contents

Introduction

It was early autumn and the blackberries were ripening on the brambles behind the whiteboard that Mr McGurk had rested up against a magnificent horse chestnut tree. I was already scanning the bush for the plumpest, darkest blackberries which were tantalizingly out of reach. I've been scratched more than an old vinyl disc when trying to reach blackberries, but that's the risk you take when searching for treasure in prickly brambles!

Mr McGurk was a teacher who changed my life. Many of us had a teacher like him, and I love the way we still call them 'Sir' and 'Miss' even after so many years. You never lose that sense of respect and reverence for what they brought to you. At school, I responded really well to teachers who approached their work slightly differently. Mr McGurk was a marathon runner and never seemed to age a day. He'd take us on a jog before class around the playing fields because he knew, from his own experience, how much it energized and enlivened the mind. For all the initial grumbling and groaning, it made us more positive and more receptive. It also drew us closer together as a group, bonded by shared happy memories outdoors in the sunshine.

Mr McGurk applied 21st-century thinking to a 1990s classroom. He knew all about working smarter, not harder. His example was a gift that kept on giving, because not only did we get to experience the positive impact of exercise and being outside – but also it encouraged us to think outside the box more. And that chimed with me as a kid who spent a lot of his childhood thinking of creative ways to deal with the difficulties I experienced reading and writing. I loved going to school, but more than anything, I wanted to be outside.

I found out that the reason I struggled so much with written work was not because I was 'dumb', but because I was dyslexic. That might have been what drew me to the world outside the classroom window. But also, some kids just prefer to be outside making something with their hands or learning among the leaves. You're much less likely to get bored outside because things are moving and changing before your eyes. You're more relaxed when you can sit where you want on the soft grass in the sunlight. You're immersed in an exciting new environment that's full of possibility. Under that horse chestnut tree in Mother Nature's classroom, I remember my bare feet on the grass, and how different the spiky shell of a conker was compared to its incredibly soft, smooth inside. I heard the calls of songbirds, the darting of dragonflies and the scuttling of beetles, and I gazed at the patterns of dappled light through the trees. I realized how connected we were to the ecosystem in front of us.

I think that the struggles I experienced inside the classroom meant that my brain compensated outside the classroom. I started being very aware of the world around me, like my uncle who developed an acute sense of hearing after he lost his sight. I realized that I was good at picking up patterns and nuances within those patterns, and that has been so helpful in my work as a cameraman. For example, when I'm outside, I'll notice a crow behaving slightly unusually and my brain is already scanning for the possible dangers a crow and her chicks might face in this environment at this time of day. I'm already expecting a peregrine falcon to appear before it does and the crow to respond by mobbing together with other crows to see off the threat. It means I'm there and I'm ready with the camera. I think the combination of having to find creative workarounds for dyslexia and the nature of what I do for a living now makes me finely attuned to behaviour, especially if it's even just a little bit out of the ordinary.

It affects the way I am around people, too. If someone's telling me everything's fine, but the words they're using somehow don't match their body language, I know something's up. It's also helped me become a good navigator: I always know which direction I'm facing and where I need to go. I like the way my brain works and I wouldn't change it. I genuinely see dyslexia as my superpower.

I was lucky to have teachers like Mr McGurk, whose guidance, encouragement and belief gave me the tools to build my own self-belief. We all just want to be included and to be believed. We all deserve the opportunity to follow our dreams. And if you give it everything you've got, you can get pretty close.

My dream was to be David Attenborough's cameraman. By the time I'd got to a position where that dream was starting to become a possibility, David had understandably dialled back his shoots on location and was spending more time in the voiceover booth. I ended up with the next-best dream coming true: one day, I received a voicemail telling me that 'David' liked the footage I'd shot of barnacle geese being hunted by white-tailed eagles. My first reaction was: 'David – I don't know a David. Oh, hang on, you don't mean. WOAAAAAHHHHH!!!!!!'

To record a sequence like that – and to have your idol, David Attenborough, narrate it – is what you live for as a cameraperson. If you'd told me as a kid that I'd be working for Sir David, I wouldn't have believed it. I still feel like a kid tearing open the wrapping paper and gazing in wonder at my first camera – a gift from my mother on my 12th birthday.

When I shot that footage, I wasn't in some far-flung and exciting-sounding part of the world like the Canadian Arctic or the South Sandwich Islands, it was just down the coast from my house in the Scottish Highlands. I think at times we can take this incredible country for granted, in the way that people often do when something is so close to home. But, you see, I wasn't born here. The UK was the far-flung and exciting-sounding place that I'd heard of as a little boy in Sudan. I think it's part of the reason why the UK will forever remain a source of never-ending wonder to me.

I love that we get to experience all of the seasons in the UK. It's something you miss when you spend a long time near the equator, where autumn, spring, summer and winter are basically meaningless. Up in the Highlands, I can't wait for that first sign of spring, when the snowdrops start peeking above the ground. That brings a smile to my face because it's the moment when we're past the coldest time of the year, but also because it tells me that nature knows best. If the snowdrops are sticking their necks out, then warmer, sunnier days are ahead. For me, summer starts when I get bitten by my first midge. And I say that with fondness, because when that midge is nibbling me, I know that the migrating bats and birds aren't going to be far behind. Autumn begins when my fingers are stained with the juice of ripe blackberries. Winter starts when I can see my breath outside. I love that I have a community that huddles together more in winter to ride out the long nights. Winter is Mother Nature's way of recharging. The ground recuperates, the rivers recuperate and the humans recuperate. There's a reason why the deciduous trees drop their leaves and the nutrients get sucked back into the roots. Everything has a rest. We work hard from spring to harvest, then enjoy the fruits of our labour throughout winter.

There's still so much I want to do outdoors in the UK. I want to hike all the hills of the west of Scotland. I want to pick up a fossil on the Jurassic Coast and find a shark tooth at the base of the white cliffs of Dover. I feel like I'm only just getting started, but I've been lucky enough to explore so much of the UK in the past few years. This book was inspired by the journeys I make between two places where I spend a lot of time: my beloved Ardnamurchan peninsula in the Highlands and Longleat Estate down in Wiltshire. The trouble is the distance between the two is 600 miles and it takes well over 12 hours to drive. I spend my life travelling almost the entire length of the country. I'm in my van more than I'm in my house. I could write a book about the merits of the different service stations around the country. And, for the record, Tebay services near Carlisle gets the gold star. It's like a National Trust version of a service station, with landscaped lakes and a wonderful panorama of the Cumbrian countryside. Frank

Skinner once said on Absolute Radio, 'If there is a road to heaven, Tebay would be the service station on that road.' He's bang on.

On my 600-mile journey, I travel across nine remarkable habitats: cities and gardens, wetlands and rivers, heathland, farmland, woodland, meadows and moorland, coastlines, the sea, and of course the Highlands. While driving my van, with Bob Marley and the *Jurassic Park* soundtrack keeping me company, I often think of the remarkable experiences, landscapes, plants and creatures I've discovered in each of the nine habitats I pass through. Over time, you start to notice things both by their appearance and by their absence. I'm thrilled that I started to see red kites in parts of England where they hadn't been seen since the 16th century. But I've also witnessed the dwindling insect population. Ten years ago, I'd have to stop the car to clear the unfortunate insects that had splattered across my windscreen, but the last time I drove from Longleat to Ardnamurchan, I don't think there was a single insect. I'm sad to say that it's symptomatic of a devastating decline in the UK's biodiversity. We've lost half of our biodiversity since the Industrial Revolution. Half!

I live my life with Mother Nature in mind as much as I can. I enjoy eating seasonally. We don't need to be able to buy blackberries every day of the year. And having something to look forward to sustains you. It's the power of delayed gratification. I long for that moment when the blackberries are ripe, and enjoy it all the more when I've waited for it. Similarly, instead of a journey being a functional solution to get you from A to B, why not take pleasure in another path – one that you haven't travelled? You'll see and hear things you've never experienced before. Instead of taking the M6 when I'm heading down south, I often drive through mid-Wales. A few years ago, I did this to see if I could chance upon the lone golden eagle that circled the Welsh valleys. I got so excited just with the possibility that I might see her. It became a quest, and when I did, she was magnificent. But when I didn't, I still had an incredible time, because I never fail to when I'm outside walking. It's where I'm at my happiest, with Midgie by my side, the collie belonging to my Scottish parents.

Some people have a glass-half-empty outlook; others prefer to see things half full. My glass is completely full, overflowing with hope and wonder. I just keep topping it up. I'm always looking up, in both senses, and it means I put myself in the best position to see something incredible. Sure, I spend time on my phone – I love watching reels on Instagram because it's a way to escape, or to be amazed by something new – but when I'm outside, I'm like the dog from the film *Up*! Everything is exciting.

The day that I stop learning about Mother Nature is the day I'm happy to meet my maker. Mother Nature has given us each a brain that's powerful beyond measure so let's use them for the right things. If there's one thing that Covid lockdowns taught us, it's how much we value the outside world. That one hour outside was the highlight of everyone's day. There were no cars on the road and the night sky became clearer. Birdsong sounded all the more beautiful because we tuned into it again. We became grateful for our green spaces once more. We realized what matters. We focused on what's important.

I wrote this book to celebrate our lesser-known creatures and plants. I'm still learning about all of them, and that's the best part of what I do. In each chapter, I've interviewed one of my favourite people, who happens to be a leading authority on the relevant family of animals or plants. I can't thank them enough for our chats, which were illuminating and joyful. And that's what being outside is all about: finding a new wonder, whether it's on your doorstep or on the journey of a lifetime, that puts a smile on your face.

Three of my favourite quotes have helped shape this book, influenced by our past, present and my hope for the future. The first is from the final letter Robert Falcon Scott wrote to his wife and their infant son on Scott's doomed return journey from the South Pole.

'I am anxious for you and the boy's future – make the boy interested in natural history if you can, it is better than games – they encourage it at some schools – I know you will keep him out in the open air.'

These words inspired his son, Sir Peter Scott, to spearhead the modern conservation movement with the founding of the Wildfowl & Wetlands Trust, to pioneer natural history broadcasting and to inspire a generation, including Sir David Attenborough, with a passion for the natural world. That letter was the touchpaper.

The second quote is a saying that emerged in the 1960s: 'The best time to plant a tree was 20 years ago. The next-best time is now.' It shows that we're playing catch-up, but it's not too late to make a difference. It also conveys its message with humour, which always manages to make a serious message stick in my mind.

The third and most powerful quote is like the antidote to the world of instant gratification. The origins of the quote are unclear, but I first heard it on the TV programme *After Life*, in a very moving scene on a park bench between Penelope Wilton and Ricky Gervais.

'A society grows great when old men plant trees the shade of which they know that they will never sit in.'

It's a beautiful sentiment. We need to leave this world in a better state than how we found it, for our children's children. One day, I want to show my children the beauty, love, fragility and resilience that Mother Nature has to offer. I want them to understand the impact we can have on the lives of future generations through the actions that we take today. I want my children to know that their dad went outside and fought for something that he thought would make the world a better place.

That journey starts as soon as we open our front doors. The view's never exactly the same day to day, wherever you are. Even outside your place of sanctuary that you know so well, you never know which of nature's marvels is going to reveal itself to you. It's all there to discover, just a short walk from your doorstep. There might be a peacock butterfly on that dandelion or a waxwing in that berry tree in the supermarket car park. Wherever I am in the world and whatever extraordinary animal or landscape I'm lucky enough to be filming, I'll get a yearning to return to Ardnamurchan. I want to see what I might be missing, especially as John Coe the killer whale always seems to turn up when I've left the peninsula! When the cameras, drones and emergency smart shirt are loaded in the back of the van, I'm almost spent, like the late-night embers on my wood-burning stove. But then I know that I'm homeward bound and that thought adds fuel to the fire.

The journey from London is going to take me 12 hours, but my job often involves spending weeks at a time in a camouflaged hide, so patience is a skill I've had to master. But we all need a little ray of light to keep us going, and fortunately, there are two moments on that long journey back home that fill up my heart. The first is when I'm approaching the sign for the Scottish border and I can't stop myself from saying, 'England, England, England . . . SCOTLAND!' when I cross it. I'm still five and a half hours from home, which is why I need a second pick-me-up towards the final furlong. And that arrives when my front wheels edge off the Corran Ferry – the gateway from Fort William to the Ardnamurchan peninsula. Everything beyond the southern shore is the work side of my life. The north side is home.

When the front wheels of my van touch that jetty, I'm finally back on my driveway. Only, it's a 44-mile-long driveway, and 38 miles of it is single-track road. So I'm just going to sit back and enjoy the most beautiful landscape on the planet. It's why, two weeks after first visiting this special place in my early 20s, I gathered my belongings into my car and drove up here for good.

Chapter 1

Cities and Gardens

———

I started thinking about this book walking around Milton Keynes, which isn't exactly my natural habitat! It's a world away from my beloved rural west Scotland home, but it's where my brother and his family live, so I come here quite a bit on my way back up from Longleat.

Milton Keynes sprang up in 1967 on what was mostly farmland in the Buckinghamshire countryside. The grid-like result feels like a geometry textbook because almost every mathematical shape is on display here: squares, circles, rectangles, ovals, even a diamond or two. There are 130 roundabouts and 20,000 rectangular parking spaces in Milton Keynes. The centre actually looks like a circuit board when you check it out on Google Maps.

But the wider city includes 5,000 acres of parkland, woodland, rivers and lakes. Around 22 million trees have been planted in Milton Keynes since 1967. That's over 75 trees per resident! Even in the city centre, I was surprised by the amount of nature on display. You just have to know where to look.

There are lots of neat lines of trees. The slight issue is many of them have been planted in a metre-by-metre square of earth next to a parking space. Back in the 1970s, it must have all looked very tidy. The trouble is nature isn't neat and tidy. Trees just want to grow big and strong, and to do that, they're going to send roots outwards to seek out nutrients and anchor the trunk. And that's going to make your neat car park look like you've installed speed bumps. It always makes me smile when I see something like that. It doesn't matter how much you try to wrestle nature into shape because life will find a way.

The centre of Milton Keynes has many horse chestnut and London plane trees. Both classically British trees, right? After all, you can't get more British than a game of conkers. But I had no idea that horse chestnuts were introduced from Turkey in the 16th century. They're actually much-loved immigrants. Horse chestnuts can grow up to 40m (130ft) tall and live for up to 300 years, but they can just about cope with a shallow root system so they're a convenient choice for cities. London plane trees aren't really from London. What?! They're thought to be a hybrid of the American sycamore and the Oriental plane, and there's something quite poetic about that. It makes them a symbol of East meets West, if you think about it. And where better for that happy meeting place than London, the home of the Prime Meridian, where the eastern and western hemispheres meet?

Half the trees in London are London planes, and they're remarkable trees. They shed their bark to rid themselves of pollutants, which is why their trunks look like they're in the middle of an exfoliation treatment. It also stops climbing plants from getting a grip and damaging them. The roots of a London plane are tough and can spread up to 15m (50ft) in all directions. That's going to make your pavement and your parking spaces bumpy. I get that in extreme cases, it can cause a serious problem for people using wheelchairs and something needs to be done. But the vast majority of the time, it just makes a pavement a bit bumpy. And what's life without a few bumps? When I see a bumpy pavement next to a tree, it tells me that in the tiny space we've given it, this magnificent tree is doing alright. I'm not keen on seeing folks cutting into a tree root to make a parking space look neater. That's why I like No-Mow May. Sure, your lawn will look neat if you cut it in May, but try giving the grass a few extra weeks and let the wildflowers grow. Then wander into your garden and count the species that you can see all benefiting from your decision. Instead of digging up the tarmac and sawing through the root, let's give the tree space to grow and support a wealth of wildlife. Taller horse chestnuts will produce more of those incredible pink and white flowers that attract bees. Caterpillars nibble the leaves, attracting birds like blue tits and great tits. Small mammals eat the conkers in autumn. I'd love it if we embraced the bumpy parking spaces. Maybe we could have a little sign near the tree that reads, 'I'm just trying to grow. And when I do, it lifts everyone up,' with bees, blue tits and squirrels perched on the letters.

As I continue my wander through Milton Keynes, I hear a chiffchaff singing its cheerful song. He's more than likely travelled here from North Africa, and it makes me think of my own journey from the banks of the River Nile to the heart of an English city, when I was eight.

We're brothers, you and I! He's happily hoovering up insects from a low tree on the edge of, you've guessed it, a car park. Like the cuckoo, a chiffchaff's song gave this little bum-wiggling warbler its name. And once someone points out that two-note song to you, it's impossible to confuse with anything else. It reminds me of a more joyful version of a car's indicator.

I notice a leaking gutter overhead that's clearly spent many years dripping water onto the corner of the street. It's transformed this unloved patch of tarmac into a mini ecosystem. A 60-cm-high (2-ft) dandelion has sprouted up, providing a welcome snack for a seven-spotted ladybird. There's a centipede nibbling away at the root, but this dandelion has weathered worse storms than that. The fact that this dandelion is here at all is a miracle. A seed must have been blown by the wind and landed in this precise crack in the ground. Sunlight and the rainfall from the leaky gutter above have fed and watered it and now it's sustaining other creatures too. It makes me wonder what Milton Keynes would look like if it was abandoned and how much greener it would become. Only, we don't have to imagine that much, because there's already a famous abandoned city that is flourishing with flora and fauna. The city's name used to be associated with disaster, but no longer.

While the full-scale ecological effects of the Chernobyl nuclear disaster aren't fully known, what is known is that nature has reclaimed Chernobyl. Even in the most highly radioactive areas of the exclusion zone – the evacuated 2,600-sq-km (1,000-square-mile) area surrounding the former nuclear power plant – vegetation returned three years after the disaster. And that's mainly because plants develop in a more flexible way than animals. They can create new cells of whichever type they need to survive. That's why a gardener just needs a stem or even a leaf of one plant to be able to grow another. But it's not just plants that are thriving there. Mammals are there too, and their numbers have boomed. There are badgers, beavers, weasels, red deer, wild boars and grey wolves. Greater spotted eagles became locally extinct after the Chernobyl disaster. By the beginning of 2022, 13 pairs were breeding within the exclusion zone. And it's mainly due to the lack of human interference.

I met a friend in Milton Keynes and while we were chatting in the street, I noticed that a crow had taken up position on the apex of an office roof to our left. It suddenly let out four 'caw' calls that caught my attention. I scanned the area for anything that could have upset the crow, but it was an ordinary city scene: road noise, conversation, the distant sound of a pelican crossing. But the crow's call had pricked up my antennae. All this was happening subconsciously while I was chatting, of course. And then, 45 seconds later, something remarkable happened. A female peregrine falcon flew past, only 10m (35ft) or so in the air. I wouldn't have guessed that peregrines would be in Milton Keynes, because they like tall buildings and the tallest here is around 50m (165ft). But I can tell you for certain that they're here! We watched her fly towards an office building, and given that I was there on 6 May, she'd probably just finished incubating her eggs. So she likely had more than one hungry mouth to feed.

In our cities, we've accidentally made the perfect habitats for peregrine falcons, and that's because tall buildings are basically just man-made cliff faces. I feel so privileged when I'm in the company of a peregrine. It's the fastest creature in the world, the Usain Bolt of birds, diving at over 320kph (200mph). And she's just there, 10m (35ft) above our heads in Milton Keynes. It's wonderful that ornithological societies and volunteers have set up live peregrine webcams, especially on cathedral spires and steeples around the country. The Englishcathedrals.co.uk website has kindly put links to ten cathedrals' webcams on the same page. I love hearing that people are watching peregrine webcams on their lunchbreaks, although one word of warning: don't have it on full volume when the church bells are about to ring!

Ten seconds after the female peregrine flew past, the crow gave four calls again. It was effectively an air-raid siren, warning other crows and nearby birds (and maybe me and my friend too!) that a hunter was approaching. And after the threat had passed, the crow gave the all-clear. This is happening every day above the streets. Sometimes you just need to gaze upwards.

My hope is that UK cities can take inspiration from other cities, like Singapore. Lee Kuan Yew, the Prime Minister of Singapore from 1959 to 1990, envisioned it as a 'garden city' in 1967. He took over during a bleak time, conservation-wise, as Singapore had lost 90 per cent of its forests, two-thirds of its native birds and 40 per cent of its mammals since it was first colonized in 1819. But things started to change rapidly. Yew oversaw the planting of over 55,000 trees between 1967 and 1970 and introduced the annual Tree Planting Day in 1971. Parks were created in the mid-1970s. In 1992, the government published their 'Singapore Green Plan' with a long-term vision to make Singapore a model green city. What they've done differently is come up with innovative ways to rewild the city, and now the city is covered in living walls and green roofs. This kind of project wins on so many levels. The air quality improves and the living walls provide shade and shelter from extreme heat. They're cooler in both senses. If you've ever been close to a living wall in a hot country, you'll have felt the difference in temperature. And they make the place look beautiful. Over half a million trees have been planted in Singapore since the launch of the OneMillionTrees Movement in April 2020. Greenery has become part of the city's cultural identity. It's become renowned around the world and has a proud legacy that its people want to uphold. That's a powerful force for good.

Wild smooth-coated otters returned to Singapore in the late 1990s, most probably swimming across from Malaysia. This has been a huge success story, not least because smooth-coated otters are listed as vulnerable on the International Union for Conservation of Nature (IUCN) Red List. It was a project 20 years in the making, since the government began cleaning the waterways in

1977. The fish started thriving, and that's when predators are going to take an interest. The otters have adapted to their new environment, inhabiting man-made structures such as voids under bridges and sewer tunnels. One family group, named the Zouk family after the nightclub they were first spotted outside, even wandered into the President of Singapore's private garden. A BBC camera crew filmed them running through a shopping complex and being given a police escort across one of the busiest roads in the city! Is it any wonder that the collective noun for otters is a 'romp'?

Singapore's otters have become a tourist attraction, and when wildlife generates that kind of international interest, everyone wants to make sure it's being properly looked after.

Wouldn't it be amazing if we had otters in the central-London stretch of the River Thames? In January 2006, when a 5-m-long (16-ft) female northern bottlenose whale was discovered swimming up the Thames through central London, it was a major news story. People lined the banks of the river to catch a glimpse. And when it became clear that Willy, as she was affectionately named (presumably after *Free Willy!*), needed help, the rescue effort was incredible. A team from the British Divers Marine Life Rescue team used a crane to gently lift her onto a barge, which then motored downriver to the Thames Estuary. By this time, news channels were providing live feeds. I remember one of the rescuers was keeping the whale's body wet with a little red watering can. It was a very moving moment.

As for otters, they're living in quite a few British cities already. That tends to surprise people when I tell them. In 1994, three otters were reintroduced to the River Itchen in Winchester. And now, otters can be seen at Winchester City Mill, a working 18th-century corn mill run by the National Trust. Volunteers have set up a camera overlooking the waterway under the mill. There's a ledge that otters jump up to after they've caught a fish. Otters have been spotted in Exeter, Colchester, Norwich, Edinburgh, Birmingham and Sheffield. Imagine how many we'd see if the water companies cleaned up their act! There are so many reasons why the state of British waterways upsets me. We can do so much better. And when we do, believe me, Mother Nature will reward us.

Every little bit helps. You could clad your own house with greenery. Think about the number of boring walls that could become wildlife refuges. I see it near the BBC site in Salford, which has become one of the most exciting places to witness urban greening. A derelict car park has been replaced with a 12-storey office building. Only, this building has the largest living wall in Europe, featuring over 350,000 plants – that's 100,000 more than Salford's population! The building's been named Eden, which makes me smile, as does its high-tech irrigation system that delivers rainwater to the plants. And pleasingly, there are still jobs that need doing by specialist gardeners. The building's being called a 'greenprint for the future', and I hope it proves to be just that. It's the perfect example of conservation and technology in partnership. And like the otters in Singapore, it's become something that people want to see. It makes you proud that something that remarkable is on your doorstep, doesn't it? The white-tailed eagles that I can see from my window are why I moved to Ardnamurchan. And I'll shout it from the rooftops!

If I was Prime Minister, I'd push forward legislation so that every new building had to be clad in greenery, with solar panels on the roof. I'd also insist on building pollinator walls, bee bricks and bee banks to provide habitats for our native solitary bees along with pesticide-free rooftop gardens with aromatic flowers and herbs that bees love, like Russian mint. It would also provide jobs in conservation and horticulture because you need bee specialists to check on the bees and gardeners to look after the roof gardens. It's also just a beautiful thing, isn't it, infusing concrete with life?

British bees are in severe decline because they've lost so much of their natural habitat. When green spaces disappear, so do bees. Around 97 per cent of our wildflower meadows have gone since the 1930s. And the plants that remain are typically sprayed with pesticides and insecticides. Climate change affects bees because they are emerging from hibernation earlier in winter, and that might not match the dates the plants are flowering. Whenever I ask kids how many species of bee are in the UK, they often answer with two (honeybee and bumblebee). And that makes sense to me – I would have said the same thing when I was that young. But there are around 270 wild bee species in the UK including 24 species of bumblebee. Only the bumblebees nest in colonies. The other bee species are solitary bees, so they build their own individual nests and work alone. They all need our help, but the fantastic thing is, it's really easy to do. Just remember that bees love the colour purple. Plants like lavender, mint, alliums and buddleia are perfect. That's not to say that they won't visit flowers of other colours though – purple is just the most visible.

Bees usually come out of hibernation in the UK in March, so what they're really going to thank you for is plants like crocuses, primroses and forget-me-nots. In early summer, bee species with long tongues will be crawling into those beautiful bell-shaped flowers like foxgloves and campanulas. And they'll all be at the nepeta (catmint) and thyme. In late summer, your garden will be a popular pitstop if you've got lavender, heather, cornflowers or buddleia. Bees don't see like humans do – their eyes detect ultraviolet light, which we can't see. But when you shine a UV light on a nectar-rich flower, something extraordinary happens. The centre of the flower (where the nectar is) appears darker, which means it's more visible to bees. It's like you or me seeing a big neon 'FOOD' sign. And leading up to the centre of the flower, you often get a pattern of light and dark spots. It's basically the ideal landing strip for a bee. Flowers do this because they rely on bees to pollinate them.

I spoke to my friend Dr Erica McAlister, a fly expert and a principal curator at the Natural History Museum, about the role that insects play in every ecosystem and the decline in insect numbers. The first time I met Erica was at a science festival in Northern Ireland. She had no idea who I was. She came over to me after I'd done a few selfies with a group of parents and kids, and I think the first thing she said to me was 'What's all the fuss with you then?!', and from that moment I knew we'd be friends. I told her I was a wildlife cameraman and we got talking about David Attenborough, who we both love above everything. She was absolutely electric and ridiculously funny. I remember her saying, 'Hamza – forget the tigers, gorillas and zebras. If you want to see sex, drugs and rock 'n' roll in the natural world, flies are where it's at.'

Erica was the one who opened my eyes to what's happening on such a small scale all around us. Insects have colonized every single habitat on earth. They even became the first animals in space, in 1947, when a bunch of vinegar flies (more commonly and confusingly called fruit flies, which actually belong to another family) were sent into space aboard a V-2 rocket captured by the Germans. The flies returned back to earth safely, much to Erica's delight (not that Erica was around yet in 1947, she'd like me to add). In 1984, we discovered that honeybees could build honeycombs in microgravity. In 2006, NASA didn't just send astronauts aboard the space shuttle *Discovery* – they sent 75 vinegar flies in special cassettes. When the shuttle returned a fortnight later, there were over 3,000 flies aboard. That's some serious excess baggage!

Vinegar flies were one of the insects I really wanted to ask Erica about because when I know for a fact that there isn't a single fly in my kitchen, how do these flies magically appear as soon as my banana starts to rot in that shameful bowl in the corner? All the doors and windows are shut! Here was her response: 'I hate to point this out to you publicly and shame you, Hamza, but you're filthy and so is your house. We all are!' You can see why they want to be inside our houses – they're warm and smell great to creatures with such an exceptional sense of smell. Plus, they can get through anything – there's no hermetically sealed house. Erica told me that they taste with their feet, can see UV light and fly around leaving each other messages everywhere. When we're watching a fly bumping into a wall or a window, they're using little supercomputers in their heads to map out their environment.

They've also been a lot more helpful to humans than many of us are aware of. Their incredible sense of smell means that they can sniff out tiny particulates of blood, and that's been instrumental in helping to solve murder cases. On a lighter note, Erica also blew my mind with the fact that flies are the pollinators of the cocoa plant. No flies, no chocolate. The flies responsible are biting midges – that's right, a relation of everyone's favourite seasonal visitor to Scotland. It's made me think about them a little differently now. We can all handle a few midge bites. We can't all handle the disappearance of chocolate!

I asked Erica about my drive from Longleat to the west of Scotland, and how I no longer need to stop and clean insects off my windscreen. Erica told me that we're seeing species loss and population crashes because 'we're stressing our poor little insects out'. They've had land use change, insecticides, light pollution, sound pollution and introduced species to worry about. She wasn't very happy about garden centres selling pretty plants that are bred for their colour and 'showy-offness' rather than for their nectar reserves. In another memorable exclamation from

Erica: 'We need local plants for local pollinators!' And then, on top of all these problems insects are grappling with, they've also got to try and handle climate change. I asked her what we could do to help them out. 'Let your garden live – don't tidy it up and make it all nice and pretty,' she said. One of the things you can do is to leave broken bits of wood, rocks and old plant pots in your garden because they're fantastic habitats for insects. Fortunately, quite a few of us, me included, seem to be doing this accidentally! Decaying leaves and compost piles are also ideal. One thing that isn't is fake grass, which accumulates bacteria and contains microplastics, which leech into the environment. What I didn't realize is that because artificial grass warms up so much, it basically boils the soil underneath, killing the insect larvae within. If these guys don't make it, there isn't as much food for the larger insects, spiders, birds, amphibians, reptiles and mammals. Fortunately, there's something we all can do. Leave your garden (or part of it) as nature intended. Plus, it'll save you time and money!

I wanted to ask Erica about some of her favourite UK insects that anyone can find in their garden, partly because I knew she'd pick something unusual, exciting and slightly terrifying. The first was the family of robber flies, which go around ambushing and assassinating other flies, grasshoppers, beetles, wasps and bees using their neurotoxic saliva. It sounds like something you'd find in the Amazon rainforest, and yet we've got 29 species of these highly venomous flies in the UK. Erica feels that they're underrepresented on our screens: 'When I'm watching a nature series (I'm looking at you, Hamza) I'm screaming at the TV because there are no insects. But we have these incredible miniature apex aerial predators on our doorstep. You don't always have to travel to the Canadian Arctic!'

The second family of flies Erica told me about was the bee flies, specifically the ones belonging to the *Bombylius* genus, which, she explained in typically poetic fashion, 'look like little fluffy flying narwhals'. I love that for Erica, these parasitic bee-mimics are the first sign of spring. Most of us would say 'daffodils' or 'blossoms', but not Erica! The males carry out complicated aerial dance moves to impress the females, and once they're joined, tail to tail, the males get dragged through the air, flying backwards helplessly. The female then aims to deposit her larvae into an unsuspecting solitary bee's nest. The adults have an incredible proboscis, like a nose, so they can access tubular flowers. This means that they're terrific pollinators, although some species do use this proboscis to stab into the bottom of the flower as a cheeky timesaver. That's why they're also sometimes known as 'flower thieves'.

★ ★ ★

Cities provide ideal habitats for many animals. The fact that cities are warmer than the surrounding countryside means that duck ponds are less likely to freeze over, for example. The waste we leave attracts scavengers. And some of these scavengers, like pigeons, are an endless supply of 'fast food', as I call them, for peregrine falcons, who are also attracted to cities. I'm writing this in a hotel room in Edinburgh and there's a herring gull nest on the roof just outside my window. Although it might not seem like it, herring gull numbers have been declining rapidly in the UK partly because their natural food source – fish – is declining in quantity and quality because of overfishing and warming seas. I've never seen a herring gull nest in the wild, and they've only been using domestic roofs for their nests since the 1940s. Our habits have created a new habitat for them.

Mammals like foxes have adapted extremely well to cities. And like herring gulls and pigeons, you can't blame them – it's easy pickings with all the scraps of food waste around. Plus, they're going to find far more rats and mice in cities than in the countryside. Without urban foxes, the number of rodents around would certainly be higher. Sometimes you hear that fox populations in cities are 'out of control', but it's nonsense. Their numbers are determined by the amount of food available and the size of their territories. Each territory is held by a lone fox or family of foxes and it can be as small as a few hundred metres squared. The resourcefulness of urban foxes is legendary. In 2011, when the Shard was nearing completion next to London Bridge station, an incredible thing happened. A male fox entered the building site, climbed the central stairwell and set up camp on the 72nd floor, attracted by the scraps of food left around by construction workers. Talk about Fantastic Mr Fox. He was eventually found, named Romeo and safely relocated to Bermondsey.

Another group of mammals that have adapted very well to cities and towns are bats, although these guys tend to get massively overlooked. It still blows my mind that there are 18 species of bat native to the UK – that's more than the number of native reptiles and amphibians combined. And when it comes to discussing and celebrating bats, I know just the person. Dr Kim Wallis is a legend in the bat world and an absolute joy to speak to. Kim is the head of nature reserves at Essex Wildlife Trust and a devoted bat carer, rehabilitating sick and injured bats to release back into the wild. At the time I spoke to her for this book, she was caring for over 25 bats including brown long-eared bats, common pipistrelles and soprano pipistrelles (the two pipistrelles were considered just one species until the 1990s) in a special bat room that she's created at her parents' farm. She keeps the baby bats at home to hand-rear because they need frequent feeds. She even takes them to work! I remember meeting Kim a few years ago and she was clutching a tiny Tupperware box. I thought it was her lunch – but it actually contained a baby bat with a tiny heated pad underneath to keep him warm.

Kim delivers amazing bat talks in schools and wildlife visitor centres across the country, and she doesn't go anywhere without the star of the show, Brad. Brad is a serotine bat, one of the largest UK bats and one of the first to emerge in the early evening. Brad's about 8cm (3in) long, which doesn't sound like a lot, but when you consider that our most common bat, the common pipistrelle, is the size of your thumb and could comfortably fit into a matchbox, he is pretty gigantic. As Kim told me, it's so helpful for people to see these two bats side by side to get the sense of how extraordinary the size variation can be with bats. I remember the first time I saw a pipistrelle, I was sure it was a baby. It was actually a relatively large adult. Here's a handy tip that Kim shared with me: 'If it's got fur, it's not a baby!'

I asked Kim about the species you'd be most likely to find in a typical garden and she told me to scan your garden about 10–15 minutes after sunset, especially between April and October. Each species has a slightly different emergence time, but the species you'll probably see most in towns and gardens are pipistrelles. If you do, it means there's likely to be a roost close by. And if you've got bats, it's a sign that you have a healthy ecosystem because bats are really important biodiversity indicators. Everything has to build from the bottom for that to happen: if you don't have the right soil conditions, you won't get the kinds of plants and grasses that attract insects. And without the insects you won't get bats.

UK bats, unlike those in other parts of the world, basically feed solely on insects, and they're struggling because of the insect decline Erica mentioned earlier. Kim told me that she's had many more starving bats requiring care this year. This means that bats are forced to group together in the few areas where prey is abundant. One such site is at their Hanningfield Visitor Centre roost (near Billericay, Essex), where there are 2,000 soprano pipistrelles – the largest colony of its kind in the UK. And while it's wonderful to be able to see that many bats, it's a bit like animals crowding around a lone watering hole in the parched African savannah. While there's relative safety there, the bigger picture is worrying.

Whenever someone tells me something worrying like that, my immediate reaction is: 'What can we do to help?' Kim told me that a lot of people don't know that attacks by domestic cats are a big problem for bats. It's one of the most common bat injuries she treats. So, if you do have a cat, keeping them in for an hour before and after sunrise and sunset can really help our struggling bats (and our birds too, for that matter!). Bats are also very sensitive to light. They're impacted by artificial lighting, especially close to where they roost or feed, because it makes them vulnerable to predation, so if you want bats to be about, put those funky lights out! You can also set up bat boxes, at least 3m (10ft) above the ground and south- or east-facing so they're exposed to the sun for some of the day.

I was curious to ask Kim about her favourite bat features, because bats are like mini superheroes, with all sorts of extraordinary adaptations. 'I've got a serious dislike of human feet, but I love bat's feet!' she told me. She went on to explain how their wings are quite similar to the human hand – they have a thumb, which is vital for climbing. And then there's the wing membrane, which Kim carefully opens up on Brad to show kids and adults. That membrane is a lot like our skin – it has the remarkable ability to heal quickly and regrow. I had no idea that the vein structure on their wing membrane is unique to each bat species and so it's a very helpful ID technique for bat workers. And then of course, there's echolocation. It turns out that it's a really amazing time to study bats because there's an evolutionary arms race going on between bats and their insect prey. Some moths are becoming increasingly able to hear the sounds bats make when they're echolocating, and so bats are adapting to make less noise in order to outsmart them. It's a constant cycle of trying to counteract each other.

This made me think of a card I received recently from a friend featuring a bat and a moth. The bat's singing 'Sweet Caroline . . .' and of course the moth can't resist going, 'Bah Bah Bah', thus revealing his location and getting gobbled up. In light of what Kim told me, it's not a million miles away from what's actually happening in gardens up and down the country!

Chapter 2

Wetlands and Rivers

———

When I think about wetlands, there's one place that springs to mind: Slimbridge. Slimbridge is a 2,000-acre wetland reserve on the River Severn Estuary between Bristol and Gloucester. And it's a big deal for so many reasons. First and foremost, it's a mecca for wildfowl. But its significance runs a lot deeper than that, because Slimbridge is widely considered the birthplace of modern conservation. It is still the headquarters of the Wildfowl & Wetlands Trust (WWT), founded just after the Second World War by Robert Falcon Scott's naturalist son, Sir Peter Scott. It was a really unusual place by the standards of the time. Firstly, instead of conducting research behind closed doors, Peter did something that was unheard of back then: he opened it up to the public. This was all the more unusual because Peter also lived there, in a house connected to the research lab. He wanted a house where he could watch his favourite birds from a comfy armchair. I'm currently writing this book watching white-tailed eagles from my rocking chair, so you can see how he and I are birds of a feather.

I hold Sir Peter in such high regard that he's one of my big five nature heroes, alongside Sir David Attenborough, Steve Irwin, Dame Jane Goodall and Dian Fossey. I was born after Peter died, but he helped guide me towards the career I chose.

Peter Scott lived an extraordinary life. His godfather was the author J M Barrie, and Peter was named after Barrie's most famous creation: Peter Pan. As a young man, Peter excelled in gliding, ice skating and sailing. He was such a strong sailor that he won a bronze medal at the 1936 Olympics in the one-man dinghy. During the Second World War, Peter won the Distinguished Service Cross for his courage and gallantry and even pioneered a unique camouflage design to help protect British ships. But the letter from his dying father steered Peter towards conservation, and after the war, he created Slimbridge.

Seven years later, Peter presented the BBC's first ever natural history programme live from his lounge. In 1961, he showcased his design skills once more, creating the famous panda logo for the celebrated organization he helped to establish: the World Wide Fund for Nature. He also invented the rocket net, used to catch birds safely so they can be recorded, tagged and treated. In 1973, he became the first person to be knighted for services to conservation. You can see why Sir Peter's pioneering work influenced the great Sir David Attenborough so much, who famously called Peter the 'patron saint of conservation'.

Slimbridge became world-renowned for its captive breeding programmes, and it's always been an incredible place to visit. The last time I was there, in early 2025, I was wearing a pair of borrowed wading trousers that were so tight they looked like I was wearing latex. No one can say I don't go the extra mile when I'm filming wildlife! My mum used to get worried about me dropping my camera when I was edging into lakes and ponds when I was a kid, so I built a floating hide using foam noodles and added camouflage netting on top. I realized that a floating hide also helps you to be at eye-level with the birds, which makes such a difference to the footage you capture. So I still build floating hides when I'm filming in wetlands, and that day at Slimbridge, I was there for the swans, moorhens and coots. I was also lucky enough to film some of the first baby ducklings of the year, and it's always a treat seeing those little golden fluff balls.

Behind the scenes at Slimbridge, there is some absolutely incredible work going on. They're at the heart of pioneering conservation and reintroduction programmes, like the one giving the critically endangered spoonbill sandpiper a fighting chance at survival. And this is all the more remarkable because *spoonies* (as these pretty little waders are known to birders) aren't found anywhere near the UK. They breed in one of the harshest environments on earth – the Russian tundra – and then winter in the wetlands of South Asia. The odds of chicks surviving to adulthood was about 15 per cent, so the folks at WWT worked hard to improve this through a technique called 'headstarting'. This involves trekking to Siberian Russia to collect eggs, which are placed in a mobile incubation unit. The eggs are transported back to Slimbridge, allowed to hatch and then hand-reared. To do that, you've got to somehow recreate their home environment and provide their traditional food source. It's painstaking work but it's paid off. Between 2012 and 2021, 82 per cent of the 309 eggs they collected hatched successfully, and 93 per cent of them went on to be released. And as is the case with many scientific projects, other species that weren't the focus of the programme, like bar-tailed godwits and Eurasian curlews, two of the UK's most beautiful birds, will benefit from the techniques that the team have learned.

Slimbridge also gave a huge helping hand to the common crane, a bird that hadn't been seen in the wild in Britain since Henry VIII was king! But sometimes you find yourself going above and beyond for the animals you love, as the fantastic Dave Paynter at Slimbridge told me on my last trip there. Dressing up in a crane costume sounds like something out of a comedy sketch, but that's what you've got to do to teach young cranes and make sure they don't become too attached to the human that raises them. Thanks to these efforts, cranes are back in the UK. They're our tallest bird, standing at 1.2m (4ft), and one of our most distinctive, with their dinosaur-like long legs, red crown and white stripe running along the side of their face and down their neck. They've also got one of the most incredible courtship dances in the animal kingdom.

It looks like something you'd see at the Royal Opera House, with pirouettes, elaborate bowing and leaps into the air. They even provide their own trumpeting soundtrack with their heads held up to the sky. I'm sure it'll inspire a *Strictly* dance at some point!

There's also a small population of common cranes in Norfolk after a successful reintroduction in 1979. One of the best places to see them is at Hickling Broad, where around 20 of them gather to roost each night for winter. I didn't know they were in Norfolk until I heard their very distinctive trumpeting call through my open van window on the way to a speaking event in Norwich. 'Am I going crazy, or is that a crane?' I said to my friend in the passenger seat. 'Yeah, there are loads here, Hamza.'

I love stories like this. Sometimes you just never know what's going to land in your garden or appear in front of you on a walk. That's why my binoculars are always around my neck. Binoculars were the first thing I packed before I came down to London to be on *Strictly* (I'm rubbish at packing). We only had Sundays off during *Strictly* and I was staying near Wembley – an unfamiliar place, surrounded by concrete. The only thing that kept me sane was heading down to the London Wetlands

Centre in Barnes with my binoculars. You can forget you're in a big city when you're there. I was surrounded by nature again. A place of sanctuary.

Another place that filled me with joy down south was the New Forest. And like the cranes in Norfolk, it was because I found something I didn't expect. Carnivorous plants. If I ask you to think of a carnivorous plant, you're going to shout 'Venus flytrap!' at me. But these incredible plants are actually only native to a tiny part of North and South Carolina in the eastern USA. If I ask people to think of a carnivorous plant native to the UK, a lot of folks think it's a trick question! But there are actually 13 carnivorous plants native to the UK. You've just got to know where to look. Three of them belong to the sundew family and are all found in wet, boggy landscapes mainly in the north and west of the UK. But you can also find all three sundew species – the round-leaved sundew, the oblong-leaved sundew and the great sundew – in the New Forest for you guys down south.

The great sundew is the rarest of the sundew species in England and Wales (although it is still widely found in northern and western Scotland) and usually only found right in the middle of a bog. The round-leaved and oblong-leaved sundews like the edges of bog pools, among sphagnum mosses. They're only about 10cm (4in) tall, with several stalks emanating from the central root (a bit like a dandelion). On the end of each of these stalks are leaves surrounded by bright red hairs. And on the end of each hair is an enticing droplet of what looks like nectar. Only this dew-like liquid is so sticky that it's like superglue to a curious insect. Once the insect is stuck, the sundew will begin to curl its leaves over the top of it, releasing digestive enzymes that dissolve the insect into a kind of nutrient soup, which the plant will absorb.

The great sundew is a distinctive and exotic-looking plant. It resembles a small hairbrush, only its bristles are red tentacles. Sadly, though, it has become incredibly rare, along with its natural habitat. Changing land use means that we've lost around 94 per cent of our peatlands and there are now only about 20 places where you can see a great sundew in the UK.

The chap who introduced me to carnivorous plants including sundews was my favourite lecturer at Bangor University, Nigel Brown. When I studied botany as part of my conservation degree, it was Nigel who took us to the exciting-sounding 'carnivorous house' at Treborth, the botanic garden that he curated from 1976 to 2015. I still instinctively call Nigel 'Sir', in the way that we do when we see our favourite teacher a decade later. A genius mind and a gentle soul, Nigel reminded me of the kind of gentleman naturalist I used to read about when I was a boy. He had a Charles Darwin meets Sir David Attenborough vibe going on.

I remember the first Nigel Brown lecture I went to at Bangor University like it was yesterday. Unlike the other lectures I'd been to by that point, this one was 100 per cent full. Nigel arrived, carrying a gigantic old slide machine loaded with 4×3 slides. He set it up on a table, pulled down the projector screen and got to work. Everyone in the audience was transfixed and he hadn't even said anything yet. It felt like he'd literally just arrived from a botany field trip in the Amazon rainforest. I could tell instantly that this was a guy who liked to get his hands dirty. And as a dyslexic who struggled in the classroom and wanted to spend time out and about in nature, that thought excited me. And it proved to be true. Field trips with Nigel were always a treat. A group of us would try and find the most obscure or tiniest plants we could to test his knowledge. 'Sir, sir, what's this one?' He'd not only recognize them instantly and give us the common name and scientific name; he would also provide an illuminating anecdote or some fascinating fact that we'd all remember. He was a one-man library. His style was also very different from the other lecturers, who would load up their lecture on PowerPoint and make their presentation available on the online portal afterwards. The fact that Nigel didn't use PowerPoint meant that his lectures weren't available online. It was very much a 'one night only' kind of gig. So you had to turn up. And turn up we did!

Nigel has this beautiful aura about him. His students loved him because he spoke from the heart and with so much knowledge and enthusiasm. That's the essence of inspiration to me. The reason I chose to study chemistry at A-level wasn't because it was my favourite subject. It was because my teacher, Mr McGurk, was so passionate and engaging. That was what made me fall in love with chemistry. Likewise, I never thought I'd fall in love with botany. If I'm honest, it was the subject I was least interested in, starting university. I was all about the big mammals, but Nigel made botany brilliant, both under the microscope and on incredible field trips, like the one we took to The Gambia with Nigel and his wife Caroline in my second year at university.

On that trip to The Gambia, I saw hippos in the wild for the first time, baobab trees and birds I'd only ever dreamed of. I remember that Clive Barlow, an ornithologist friend of Nigel's based in The Gambia, set us students a challenge to mimic a particular West African bird. The prize on offer: a pint. I mean, we were university students, after all! I'd been practising bird calls since I was about seven, so I waited for the right moment, when Clive's back was turned, and really went for it on the bird call. Clive suddenly turned around, expecting to see the bird! I don't drink, so I didn't collect my prize, but I did celebrate with both arms raised like I'd just stuck the landing in an Olympic gymnastics event.

Anyway, let's migrate back from the African savannah to the carnivorous house at Treborth. For this book, I asked Nigel what it is about carnivorous plants that fascinates people. 'They're rule-breakers!' he said. 'Because plants are supposed to be producers, not consumers.' Carnivorous plants are also specialists in thriving in adversity. They often live in waterlogged habitats starved of elements like nitrogen and phosphorus, so they catch and digest insects to supplement their diet.

The most common carnivorous plant on our islands is the round-leaved sundew, which Nigel described to me with bubbling joy. 'It's got these lovely little tennis racquet-like leaves; each little leaf, which is only a centimetre across, has around 1,000 glands.' He then described something that makes you see the world in a completely different way: looking at a plant like the round-leaved sundew under a microscope. Suddenly, the beautifully vivid colours and structures come to life and the plant moves if you touch it. It's extraordinary. I asked him what's going on in the plant once an insect becomes trapped in the sticky dew. 'Ah, Hamza, we don't know the full story, but it's almost certainly to do with an electrical and chemical change in the gland that causes the stalk of each gland to start bending inwards towards the centre of the leaf.' After that, the contents of the glands, which are full of enzymes, explode out over the insect, which suffocates it. Then they begin to digest it. Pretty gruesome but mighty effective.

Nigel brought up another group of carnivorous plants that he described as 'even more remarkable'. And they're a group that often get overlooked, which is exactly why

I wanted to talk about them in this book. They're the bladderworts, and we have seven species in the UK, all of which lurk about in fens and swamps. Once again, Nigel's eyes lit up and he told me there are quite a few to be found in Anglesey. They work in a different way to sundews. Instead of a sticky prison, they have a trap door. Little sensitive hairs on their leaves guide aquatic insects such as water fleas towards the trap door, 'much like a sheep pen', as Nigel explained. The hinge for the trap door is a trigger hair and that's sensitive to the tiniest movement. Then, within five milliseconds, the chamber fills with water. It's remarkable how quickly these mechanisms can work in plants, which you usually associate with being graceful and gradual. That's not the most remarkable thing about them, though. It turns out that a community of microbes lives inside the traps which also feed off the insects and release nutrients, which the plant uses. 'It's an extraordinary ecosystem in miniature,' Nigel told me, always saving the best until last.

★ ★ ★

I'm very lucky doing what I do because I meet a lot of kids, and the way they think fills me with wonder. When kids see a newt up close, they often ask me, 'Is it a little dinosaur?'

Whenever I see Toothless from the *How to Train Your Dragon* films, I think of a newt. That's because he was based on a giant salamander, and the newt is a member of the salamander family. So newts are cool – they made it to Hollywood! – but as a friend told me recently, they do have a PR problem.

'It's just a rubbish name, isn't it – newt? Newt sounds like the kind of sound you make when you're sighing,' he told me. I got what he was saying.

'Okay, what about underwater dragon. Or aquadragon?' I suggested. 'Now you're talking, my man!' he answered. Since then, I call newts underwater dragons. I even 'correct' people who say 'newt'. I'm hoping that if I do that enough times over my lifetime, the name will stick! There is a serious point to make about names, though. How much cooler does the name 'lammergeier' sound than 'bearded vulture'? It makes it sound legendary, and that can make a big difference when it comes to building awareness. And there needs to be more of that with newts, because they're incredible.

We've got three species of newt native to the UK. The smooth newt (also called the common newt) is the most widespread, followed by the great crested newt. And one of the largest populations of both of these species in the UK is in the outskirts of Peterborough. The area around Peterborough has huge deposits of clay, which has been used to make bricks. Peterborough became famous for brick-making in the 19th and 20th centuries. When the clay extraction company moved out of Orton Pits in the 1990s, nature moved in (again). The excavations at the site had left 300 undulations. Over time, these became ponds. The 145-hectare site is now an SSSI (site of special scientific interest) and an SAC (special area of conservation). Up to 30,000 adult newts live here. It also has ten species of stonewort, which look like plants but are actually complex algae. One of the ten species is critically endangered and was thought to be extinct in England. But it was found here.

I also studied great crested newts when I was at university in north Wales. These guys look the business, with their bumpy black bodies, jagged crests, gold rings around their eyes and funky bright-orange bellies with black polka dots. This pattern is as unique as a fingerprint. I realized that we also have something in common: we both like dancing. The male's courtship display is straight out of *Strictly*. They stand on their front legs, arch their backs and wave their tails in the air like they just don't care. We were on one of those exciting night-time expeditions with torches which make you feel like you're in the SAS, only it's the Special Animal Service and you're there counting newts. I remember the landscape looking like no-man's land in the First World War – it was all undulations and holes filled with water. When I shone my torchlight on a mama newt, she had just laid her eggs and was very carefully using her hind legs and feet to wrap one in a leaf. I was giddy with excitement. I was a 19-year-old acting like a 5-year-old, and I would still feel the same way today!

One of the reasons I get excited about newts is because they're a bioindicator – a vital species that can be used as an indicator for the health of an ecosystem. If you've got newts in your pond, it means that the water's clean and there's a good food source for them. They're all signs that you're looking at a healthy habitat and that's what we want to see. There are smooth newts in the pond near my parents' house in Northampton and I love going to check up on them. 'I'm just off to see the smooth newts, Mum,' I call as I head out the door. Then I hear the start of the conversation between my mum and my dad as I'm walking down the garden path.

'What did Hamza say?' my dad asks.

'He's going to see the . . . er, you know, those little lizardy things,' my mum answers.

'They're smooth newts, guys!' I shout towards the house, amused and exasperated in equal measure. As I said, they wouldn't have this problem if they were called underwater dragons!

* * *

Of all the creatures that live in our waters, the European eel might be the most misunderstood. It's also one of the most underrated. When you discover the journey they've taken just to get to the UK, you'll see them in a completely new light – because these guys give the Arctic tern and the Brownlee brothers a run for their money in the endurance stakes.

If you think about what kind of creature an eel actually is, you'd be forgiven for scratching your head. Is it a snake? Some kind of ray? A mega-worm? Eels are actually fish – a really elongated fish with a snakelike head and body and some pretty cool characteristics. The first thing you notice when you try to handle one is that they're pretty much impossible to pick up – like a wet bar of soap sliding around a bathtub! That's because eels are covered in slime, which works as a clever protection mechanism. It helps them avoid being caught but also provides a barrier to parasites that try to enter their bodies through the scales. It also helps wounds to heal. Adult eels can actually survive out of water, and they can slither out of rivers and into fields, where they'll start feasting on slugs and worms. The first time you see it, you think they're drowning until you realize that they're basically gorging themselves at a takeaway joint. It's incredible to watch, but sadly, it's now a very rare sight. And that's because eels are one of our rarest creatures, declared critically endangered by the IUCN since 2008. They're also one of the most mysterious, because for centuries, no one knew where they actually came from.

This mystery was finally unravelled in 2022 when scientists caught adult eels in the Azores and fitted them with satellite tags. This confirmed something that had been suspected for centuries: European eels travel to the Sargasso Sea (an area of the western Atlantic Ocean) to breed before dying. The Sargasso Sea is one of the most extraordinary parts of the world's oceans. The only sea in the world that doesn't touch any landmass, it's instead bordered by four strong ocean currents (one of which is the Gulf Stream) that together form one big clockwise current called the North Atlantic Gyre. This system of currents leaves a big oval shape at its heart: the Sargasso Sea. Think of it like the eye of a storm. Everything's moving frantically around it, but the eye itself is calm. The Sargasso Sea is known for its still waters and lack of wind and is named for the seaweed (belonging to the genus *Sargassum*) that floats in huge accumulations on the surface.

After the eels lay their eggs, the babies drift across the Atlantic, catching a ride on the Gulf Stream and beginning an epic 6,500-km (4,000-mile) ocean voyage towards Europe. It takes them around three years. And during that time, they change dramatically from eggs to larvae to transparent, fragile young eels, known as glass eels. At this point in their life cycles, you can see their hearts and red gills clearly. These glass eels head towards freshwater rivers, lakes and streams and look for a safe place to catch crustaceans, worms and insects and start transitioning into juveniles (elvers). They darken and mature, and their bellies become yellow, so they're known as yellow eels at this point. And they'll stay in this stage of their life cycle, gradually growing for up to 20 years. It's only when they're ready to breed that they turn silver and are ready for their final voyage, 6,500km (4,000 miles) back to the Sargasso Sea.

And if their epic voyage at the beginning and end of their lives wasn't enough, they've had a rough ride with humans. They became a staple of the working classes in the UK, and by the 18th century, they were appearing in pies in the East End of London. On a Sunday, pleasure steamboats took East Enders over to the posher west of London where the air was cleaner and everything greener. And these tourists still wanted their eel pies for lunch, so an inn appeared on a crescent-shaped islet in the Thames near Richmond. The inn served one dish: eel pies. So the pub became Eel Pie House and the island was named Eel Pie Island. Jellied eels became the classic Cockney dish and you'll still find them on the menu in old-school pie and mash shops in south and east London. But unlike in the 18th century, none of the eels come from the Thames – they're all imported.

The last 40 years have witnessed a staggering 95-percent decline in the number of eels reaching European waters. Like many things to do with eels, the cause isn't entirely understood, but it's likely to be a combination of illegal fishing, chemical pollution, reduced water quality, altered water levels and a possible parasite problem. And the ones that do make it here don't exactly have it easy, needing to contend with weirs, dams and sluice systems on our rivers (and hydroelectric dams too, but mostly in Europe). There are thought to be 2,000 barriers to eel migration in the Thames river system alone. It's amazing that eels can deal with any of these. They've been filmed shimmying up dam walls; if the surface is rough and wet enough, they'll get over it. I remember seeing footage of a whole column of elvers climbing up a waterfall on the River Ness. These guys have made a serious effort to get here, and we need our eels, because they have a vital part to play in maintaining healthy wetlands and rivers, feeding on dead animals and bugs, recycling nutrients and providing a food source for herons, bitterns, ospreys and otters.

After travelling thousands of miles to get to the UK, eels often travel upstream into rivers. The trouble is, we've made so many alterations to the natural landscape to suit our needs, and rivers are one of the most greatly affected features. They've been straightened, widened, deepened, diverted, dammed, culverted and embanked. We've stopped them from doing what they're meant to do, and that ultimately bites us in the backside.

Rivers were straightened during the Industrial Revolution to make them more navigable, to create more usable land alongside them and to stop particular areas from flooding. The trouble is, you end up with a faster-flowing river and that completely changes the landscape and the animals and plants that rely on it. Plants struggled to take root and fish couldn't use sections of the river as spawning grounds. Faster-flowing water also picks up more sediment from the riverbed, and that's going to end up being deposited somewhere downstream. With less sediment and a faster river, you've also got a serious problem when it comes to flooding. Sure, the area that's been straightened is going to be alright, but you'll end up with an area of land that's going to experience much worse flooding than the river had before it was straightened. It's just relocating and amplifying a problem.

The thing is, we're not in the Industrial Revolution anymore. We don't need rivers to be faster or wider because we're not transporting barges full of coal, iron ore and timber. What we need is to 're-wiggle' them. What's not to like about that word?! It makes me break into a kind of joyful dance. Re-wiggling involves creating meanders to restore the river to how it used to look, and more importantly, to restore the habitat that it used to sustain. In a fast-flowing river, you've either got to find a way to cling to the riverbed or swim super-fast up it. With meanders, the river moves slower and that environment supports much more biodiversity. Re-wiggling also presents an opportunity to re-establish the former floodplain of the river, and that will provide a wonderful refuge for wildfowl. So a half-mile section of straight, fast-flowing river can be completely transformed into an ecosystem teeming with wildlife. Let's get started I say!

Yes, there are hoops you need to jump through to get the green light for a re-wiggling project. Fortunately, we're lucky enough to have a creature in the UK that bypasses the need to conduct surveys, negotiate with landowners and gather funds. The beaver. I spend many weeks of the year at Longleat Estate in Wiltshire, where I'm lucky enough to film (and co-present) *Animal Park* with the lovely Ben Fogle, Kate Humble, Megan McCubbin and some of the finest rangers, keepers and vets around. We have animals from across the world at Longleat including several endangered species. But when I'm taking a break from filming, there's only one animal I'm heading straight for, and that's the pair of beavers. And it's because, unlike the other incredible animals at Longleat, they haven't been brought here. They just appeared one day in 2021!

The beavers moved into the estate's famous water feature, Half Mile Lake, which we couldn't believe, because at that point in time, it was also home to two hippos. Before Sonia and Spot very sadly passed away, both aged 49, in 2023 and 2024, they were coexisting quite happily with the beavers. The hippos would turn in for the night, and then the beavers turned up! This was all the more amazing because the last time beavers and hippos shared the same habitat was over 100,000 years ago, when this area would have been a gigantic interglacial swamp.

The beavers set to work as soon as they got to Longleat, building dams and lodges. A small stretch of stream is now a network of ponds, brimming with native wildlife. They've transformed the landscape and it's an absolute privilege to have watched that every tail swish of the way. Half Mile Lake looks for all the world like a natural lake, but it was actually hand-dug in 1790 and made both to imitate and to support nature. The beavers are the real deal. They're like Mother Nature's landscape gardeners, building biodiversity wherever they go. And they've added more numbers to their construction team at Longleat because in the summer of 2024, we saw the footage that we'd all been hoping for: beaver babies had been born!

Contrary to what you see in cartoons, beavers do not use their tail to pat down mud, but they do slap their tails as a way of signalling oncoming danger to other beavers. Their tail also acts as a rudder in the water to help them steer, and on land, it helps them balance. It's also a fat resource, a bit like a camel's hump. The urban legend that beavers' testicles have medicinal properties isn't true, and neither's the one about beavers biting their own testicles off when they're being pursued and flinging them towards the hunter! What is true is that they have special sacs near their bums, which secrete a fluid called castoreum that they use to mark their scent and to help waterproof their fur. Castoreum was thought to be a kind of medical cure-all in medieval times. When people started realizing that it didn't actually work, other uses were found. Whoever first thought it could be used in perfume making or to add a 'vanilla' flavour to dairy products and desserts must have been slightly unhinged, but the trend took off and castoreum was still being used in this way into the 1980s. In the 1930s, synthetic alternatives were developed to recreate the aroma because, for some reason, it seems that humans are drawn to the unique fragrance produced by the sacs near a beaver's rear end!

Right, let's move on swiftly to the other end of the beaver. Beavers' teeth are constantly growing and are self-sharpening. A team of researchers only recently discovered (in April 2024) that beavers' teeth aren't the distinctive orange-brown colour they are because they contain iron-rich materials in the enamel. The colour actually comes from a thin surface layer on the incisors made up of aromatic amino acids and inorganic minerals. What they do with these teeth is just extraordinary. They don't actually eat all the way through a tree trunk, though. And that makes sense, because at that 'Timber!' moment, the last place you want to be is next to the trunk. Younger beavers sometimes make this mistake, but they learn their lesson pretty quickly after frantically scampering to safety. Adult beavers just keep nibbling, and checking. When there's not much holding the tree up anymore, you'll see them sit down and listen. They're waiting for the tell-tale cracking sounds. When they hear those first few cracks, they leave and come back the next day. Wisdom comes with experience!

They fell trees for lots of reasons, not least because they can't climb and so can't nibble the tasty leaves at the top any other way. In their natural environment, felling trees isn't a problem. It's only an issue when they fell trees in close proximity to man-made structures like paths, farmland, roads and bridges. We always hear that beavers are 'ecosystem engineers' but that phrase has been so overused that I wanted to come up with something better. 'Mother Nature's landscape gardeners' was the best I could come up with. It was Sophie Pavelle from the Beaver Trust who perfectly described the impact of beavers felling trees. She said, 'When a beaver fells a tree, it doesn't kill it – it simply turns it from an upright, vertical structure into a horizontal 'shrub' that continues to grow and provide refuge for lots of other species.' Felling a few trees actually allows more trees to grow. As for the fallen tree, it starts to create a series of interconnected ecosystems. The wood will decay and produce a habitat for fungi and invertebrates. That, in turn, provides a food source for amphibians, reptiles, birds and fish. Deadwood in the water provides shelter from predators and becomes a breeding site for fish. In a few years, the whole area becomes a richer, more biodiverse habitat. All because the beaver has felled a tree.

And a diverse ecosystem gets to the heart of what I love about nature: there are so many weird and wonderful parts to it. But not only that – it's that it all works together in a beautiful circle of life. But it's no secret that I've always had a soft spot for birds. And it was in my 20s in north Wales where my love for birding really took off.

Chapter 3

Heathland

———

In my early 20s, I'd just started ringing birds, and I was completely hooked. Bird-ringing involves safely catching birds and placing a lightweight, uniquely numbered ring around one of their feet. It allows us to monitor their physical characteristics like weight, wing length and sex, as well as their movements, feeding behaviour and longevity. It's been an extremely helpful tool to unlock some of the mysteries of migration. It's one thing watching birds from a distance, but ringing allows you to examine these little winged marvels in detail. It fills you with immense respect for the epic migration journeys many of them undertake just to get here, especially when some of them weigh about the same as a 50p coin.

One of my first bird-ringing trips was to north Wales with my friend Tony Cross. We spent quite a bit of time climbing up trees and ringing choughs, herons, egrets – the lot. It was just fantastic. At the end of the day, Tony asked me if I wanted to go nightjar ringing. I thought he was winding me up at first – teasing the newbie – because I'd been a birder since I was a kid and I'd never heard of anyone ringing a nightjar. It's hard enough to even see a nightjar when it's right in front of you let alone be able to get close enough to ring one. But it turns out Tony was serious. I was on board, whenever and wherever he was talking about!

I got a message from him a couple of weeks later at about 4pm. It was just a set of coordinates. Then another message pinged up.

'Can you be there in four hours, Hamza?'

'Roger,' I said.

I arrived at RSPB Arne in Dorset – which is, by the way, one of the best places in the country to hear and see nightjars – and found myself in an area of straggly heathland. It looked a bit like a farmer had run through the field with a horribly lop-sided mower, tearing chunks out of the earth and leaving clumps everywhere. But as I looked over the landscape, it struck me that this is exactly the kind of habitat nightjars love because the colours, textures and densities match their feathers perfectly. And when I say 'perfectly', I'm not exaggerating in any way. After we'd set up our position, we stayed motionless, waiting. After a while, Tony nudged me.

'There's one,' he whispered, indicating a spot about 50 yards to my left. I scanned every square inch of land and couldn't see anything. So Tony started describing the patch I was supposed to be looking at, in increasingly painstaking detail.

'There's a twig pointing at a 90-degree angle – do you see that?'

'Ah, okay, I think I've got the twig – the one with the stone next to it, right?' I said, slightly desperately.

'That's not a stone, Hamza. That's the nightjar!'

When I realized what I was actually looking at, it felt like I'd finally solved one of those Magic Eye puzzles. I'd never have spotted it if it wasn't for Tony. But now I can pass on what I've learned to others. I can help provide that moment of magic when you see your first nightjar on the ground. Because these guys are unlike any other creature on the planet. In fact, it almost feels like they're from another planet.

At dusk, male nightjars make an incredible sound known as 'churring'. It has the regularity of a cricket but then the frequency shifts up and down, a bit like the noise you get when you're trying to find a station on an FM radio. It basically sounds like you're in a sci-fi movie. And then, the nightjar takes off from its perch (not that you'll actually see it), still churring, and makes these short, sharp, snapping noises as it whips its wings up and down, known as wing claps. With its pointed wings, long tail and almost hovering motion, it looks like a kind of night kestrel.

Suddenly Tony pulled a handkerchief out of his pocket and started flapping it around above him. I literally had no idea what he was doing. It was near the summer solstice though, so I genuinely thought he'd broken into some kind of celebratory Morris dance. But then I saw a black silhouette just above us and a little white flash against the dark grey sky behind. That little flash was the white patch on the male nightjar's outermost tail feathers (he's also got another white patch near the top of his wings). By flapping a white handkerchief, Tony was mimicking that white flash, so of course, the male nightjar thought that another male was displaying on his patch. So he was patrolling the sky trying to beat him up!

Fortunately, Tony and I were with wildlife cameraman Mark Yates, who had brought an SLX-SuperHawk with him – a long-range thermal-imaging camera. And you really need a special bit of kit to film such a special bird in the fast-approaching pitch-black of night in the countryside. The SuperHawk captured incredible detail of the whiskers on both sides of the nightjar's beak. They act as a kind of funnel, directing insects towards its beak. It reminded me a little bit of a pair of wicketkeeper's gloves, which give you a better chance of catching a cricket ball in flight. The nightjar has a special serrated middle claw, which works like a miniature moustache comb. And then it has these larger-than-you'd expect dark eyes that look like they glow in the dark. They don't actually – it's a mirror-like structure called the *tapetum lucidum* (Latin for 'shining tapestry') behind the retina (the layer at the back of the eye). It works by reflecting the light rays that the retina didn't pick up the first time and sending them back to the retina. You also find this structure in another group of birds that specialize in hunting at night: owls. It gives them much better night vision than we have.

Their camouflage is their best form of protection, and to be fair, when you manage to evade a trained cameraman looking directly at you, it's a pretty decent defence. During the day, they sit absolutely still, crouching low to the ground if they feel threatened with eyes half closed. The only predator that's going to detect them is a fox who happens to be walking towards them. They'll flush (take flight suddenly) when the fox is within a couple of metres, and that is sometimes enough of a distraction so the fox won't find the chicks, if the nightjar has them.

Any winged creature that comes out at night has a bad rep, barn owls and bats especially, for being associated with evil spirits. It's funny, though: old wives' tales seem to spare cuddly looking nocturnal mammals from this association. No one's ever heard of a spectral hedgehog or a demon badger, have they?! Before the 17th century, nightjars were called 'goatsuckers' because of a tale about them flying at dusk suckling on goats' udders. Of course, that wasn't a sinister enough myth for a strange-looking nocturnal bird, so they added in a bit about poisoning the goat, causing its udders to fall off and making it go blind. Before bursting into flames and making the sign of the antichrist. (Okay, I made that last bit up!)

They've also had a more poetic nickname, thanks to the writer Thomas Hardy, who described one as a 'dewfall-hawk'. He must have chosen the name because nightjars hunt in that mysterious time of the night when the dew forms. But dark myths are powerful forces, and they don't even evaporate when confronted with evidence to the contrary. I think we want to believe scary stories, like the sailor's superstition that storm-petrels are the ghosts of drowned sailors. And I can understand why; before the age of lights, cameras and Google, when you're travelling a vast open ocean in the dead of night and you hear an unearthly noise, your imagination's going to be flapping around this way and that. And to be fair, a storm-petrel's call isn't a far cry from the creaking timbers of a boat, which probably did sound like footsteps as the bird got closer to the sailor, who was no doubt thinking, 'This is because I sin and the ghosts are after me!'

I love recording animals in new ways and learning in intricate detail about their anatomy and behaviour. But I also love learning about the old terminology people used when they didn't have access to modern technology. The fact that nightjars were called goatsuckers tells you they were hanging around goats at the time of year when kids are born. That means that you're going to see them from late spring and into the summer. It must be to do with a likely food source that's plentiful around animals and their young, especially at dusk: insects. The fact that these birds are seen flying at dusk indicates that they'll probably have large and especially interesting eyes. And the fact they chase insects means they're going to have to be fast and quite acrobatic. All this helps create a picture of the bird before you've even seen one. You might be able to tell that I get really excited by this kind of deduction work and by encouraging other people to think in the same way.

RSPB Arne has become a wonderful nightjar hotspot, with 60 territorial males found in 2023 (thanks to the diligent work of bird-ringers). You can see why it's the ideal spot, with open areas of heathland and woodland edges, so nightjars can perch, completely camouflaged against the branches of trees. So look out for overgrown grassy heathland areas, especially in southern England but also in Wales, northern England, Norfolk and southern Scotland between May and August. Hearing a nightjar for the first time is special. It's such a unique and incredibly otherworldly experience. If you're lucky and you scan the landscape slowly, you might just see one. Double-check that knobbly bit of bark or grey/brown stone!

* * *

At first glance, heathland looks like natural wilderness, with its low scrubby vegetation, but this landscape was actually formed by humans. We cut down the trees on soil that wasn't useful for growing crops and let animals in to graze. That made the soil more acidic, which suited plant species like heather, gorse, bracken and grasses. Unfortunately, because much of it seems like a wilderness, it was a prime candidate for agricultural and commercial development in the 20th century. That was terrible news for our rarest reptile: the secretive smooth snake, because these guys like nothing better than the warmth, cover and rich pickings that heathland provides.

The smooth snake is a constrictor. I love telling people that, because everyone starts imagining some kind of enormous python, but in fact, the majority of snakes kill their prey by constricting them. It's just that in the UK, the smooth snake is the only one. They hunt rodents and smaller reptiles, including the slow worm, and are completely harmless to humans. It does look a bit like an adder and is a similar size, but the tell-tale sign is the lack of black zig-zag marking on its back. They're quite common in Europe, but it's a different story here in the UK where they're restricted to specific heathlands in Hampshire,

Dorset and Surrey. Small numbers were successfully reintroduced to West Sussex in 1997 and Devon in 2010. But its long-term survival depends on us setting aside heathland and protecting it. Fortunately, there are some fine folks on the case.

Snakes in the Heather was a project led by Amphibian and Reptile Conservation (ARC) in partnership with several conservation organizations. It helped engage the public in communities next to smooth snakes' heathland habitat, coordinated a monitoring programme which found smooth snakes in areas they'd never been recorded before and directed contractors and volunteers to restore suitable habitats. It also set up the ARC Survey Hub, which makes monitoring and recording reptiles in the UK easier, so even though the project has ended, it'll have a lasting legacy.

I'm always encouraged when I hear about these kinds of conservation efforts because I have a soft spot for reptiles. In fact, one of my first jobs was working in a reptile shop. One day when I was behind the counter, I remember a panic-stricken man rushing in.

'I've managed to trap an escaped snake – I think it's a corn snake – in a cardboard box,' he said. 'Can we bring it round to you?'

'What does it look like?' I asked.

'It's green,' he answered.

Now if there's one thing a corn snake isn't, it's green, being conspicuously bright-red and orange.

I could have bet my binoculars that this fella was going to be a grass snake. Ten minutes later, a cardboard box arrived on the counter. I carefully peeked inside and saw this beautiful little snake, coloured like a pair of combat trousers, with its dark-green, brown and black colouring except for the tell-tale yellow patches on its neck like a shirt collar. 'That's a grass snake,' I said. 'Where did you find it?'

'On our lawn,' he answered.

'Have you got a big pond or something like that near you?' I asked.

'Yeah – there's a kind of lakey area on the other side of our back fence.'

'Right – he'll be living in that, so get yourselves over the fence with the box and let him out by the lake. He'll probably slither straight into it.'

He paused for a second. 'Grass snakes swim?!' he asked.

I nodded, smiling. 'Bloody good at it, too.'

People don't tend to know this about grass snakes until they've actually seen one. When most people imagine a swimming snake, they tend to think of an anaconda (thanks, Hollywood) or highly venomous black and white sea snakes, but all snakes can swim. Some just do it a lot better than others. Grass snakes are amazing swimmers, moving across water in the same S-shape as on land. They're our most common snake in the UK, but you won't find them in Scotland or Northern Ireland. I saw my first one in my parents' garden, appearing out of the water like a submarine, and taking down a frog, who looked as surprised as I was.

The subject of snakes reared its head on the open day I went to at the University of Bangor, where I went on to spend many happy years. I was introduced to a zoology professor called Wolfgang Wüster. His is the kind of name you never forget, especially because it sounds like the alter-ego of a Marvel superhero. He asked me why I wanted to come to study at Bangor – in fairness, it's the one question I really should have been prepared for. I fumbled around with an answer about loving the wildlife in north Wales, but I was a bit nervous and wasn't thinking straight, so I sidestepped and asked him what his speciality was. Everything about him seemed to instantly change. His eyes lit up and he said: 'Sssnakes!'

Professor Wüster's answer was loaded with excitement and a kind of showmanship, as though he'd just told me he was a magician. Then he just couldn't stop himself from telling me about a particular type of snake that hissed in a really unusual way. It didn't hiss like other snakes do, by letting air pass through the glottis – a small piece of cartilage in the throat. Then I realized that I knew exactly which snake he was talking about. It was a species of saw-scaled viper that's found in north-east Africa, where I was born. The snake 'hisses' by rubbing its scales together in order to preserve moisture that it might lose by actually hissing. Professor Wüster was utterly delighted that I knew what he was talking about, and to be honest, I think that was the only reason I got into the University of Bangor at all!

★ ★ ★

I'd occasionally seen grass snakes in the UK when I was young, but it wasn't until I moved up to Scotland that I saw my first adder. Adders love a wild garden, especially my neighbour Joyce's place. She's followed my advice to set aside a beautiful area of organized chaos. It's got all these nooks and crannies, and it's become a wonderful wildlife haven. One day I popped over and found Joyce gardening. I couldn't help but notice an adder about three feet away from her.

'Er, careful, Joyce, there's an adder just to your left.'

'Oh yes, I know,' she said casually. 'There's another one here as well,' she said, pointing to her right. 'Ooh, and there's one right behind you, Hamza.'

I love it when people embrace nature. I also love it when people realize that they don't need to sacrifice much in order to let nature thrive. Joyce and her husband Richard are very pleased that their garden has attracted adders. Their grandchildren come to stay, and they're all out there with magnifying glasses talking in hushed voices so they don't scare away the snakes. It's one of my favourite things to witness – a love of nature taking root. None of Joyce's family are scared of the adders, because they know how to recognize them and they know what the adders are seeking. They just want to warm themselves up in the sun in and around the dry-stone wall and occasionally find a nice juicy rodent. Job's a good 'un. As Joyce tells me: 'They're not interested in harming us – they just want to use our garden.' The only minor sacrifice is that they keep their dog out of the back garden for part of the day when the sun's shining, but there's lots of other space for everyone to enjoy.

Yes, adders are venomous, but they're quite timid creatures. They're also a lot smaller than most people assume, only growing to about 60cm (2ft). They basically just want to keep themselves to themselves. The only time an adder might bite is if they feel no option but to defend themselves. And that's if they're surprised by a dog or if someone accidentally stands on them in long grass. And even then, most adder bites on humans and dogs are 'dry' bites (i.e. without venom) because their venom is precious. It costs them a lot of energy to produce and inject that venom so they want to use it on something they can actually eat, like a rodent rather than a dog or a person. Adders aren't the villains that snakes have been made out to be. They're also not the top of the food chain in the UK.

There are two creatures that hunt adders in the UK: the buzzard and the long-eared owl. But there's also a third bird of prey that catches them – the golden eagle – and I was able to tell my herpetologist friend Nigel Hand about that discovery when we were chatting for this book. I think it was the first time I'd been able to tell him something about snakes that he didn't know! I told Nigel that my fellow cameraman and friend Steve Phillips showed me his footage of a goldie catching 16 adders in a single day on the Isle of Mull and bringing them back to its nest for its chick. It was extraordinary footage.

Nigel probably knows more about snakes in the UK than anyone else and I really wanted to ask him why he'd fallen for the scaly things. It always fascinates me why people fall in love with a particular animal, especially when it's a little niche, and, in my experience, there's often an unusual story behind it. Nigel told me that it was because 'he loved the unloved', which is something that has really stuck with me. He said that rather than heading to the gorillas, lions or penguins at the zoo, he'd be straight off to the reptile house. Before long, he wanted to see snakes in the wild. Nigel's parents, bless them, would drop him off at an adder site when he was barely in double digits and he'd spend the whole day happily on his own. I basically had exactly the same experience, only the animals I spent the day looking for were feathery rather than slithery.

Nigel discovered he had a knack for finding snakes, honing his skills on grass snakes, which were quite widespread where he grew up, close to the canal network of the Midlands. He told me that one summer, during school holidays, he found over 100 grass snakes, but what eluded him was adders, which were quite rare in that landscape. He put his thinking cap on, scouted about and deduced that one place they might be was in an area of woodland close to his secondary school. 'And that's where I had my first encounter with an adder – at break time! I found two on a bank and it felt like nobody in the world knew they were there except me,' he told me, reliving the moment that changed the course of his life. So that's where Nigel would disappear to at lunchtime, to check up on his adders. He told his rural science teacher and biology teacher about his discovery, but they genuinely didn't believe him. So he marched them off to the site, and, sure enough, to the amazement of his teachers, there were two adders on the bank.

Nigel told me he'd gone back over 30 years later to that site when he was commissioned to conduct an adder survey. The surrounding landscape had completely changed, with new housing built close by. The adders had vanished. It made Nigel realize that when he saw them as a child, those adders were living right on the edge.

One area that Nigel used to visit regularly as a kid – a heathland site on the fringes of Wolverhampton – has fared much better. That's thanks to the National Trust, who Nigel works with, and their passionate local volunteers.

Nigel started using his remarkable radio-tracking skills there, attaching transmitters to adders to follow their movements and learn about what they need to survive. He told me how different our approach is now compared to the 1970s and 1980s when ecology just wasn't a thing. Back then, housing developments went ahead and ploughed vast areas up, which would have killed the adder population. It was only really in the 1990s that people realized that wildlife was something we've got to look after and preserve.

The kind of job that Nigel wanted as a young man didn't exist yet. But snakes were never far from his thoughts. While studying art at university, where he met his future wife, Nigel became a talented rug-weaver, incorporating reptile designs into his work. In his time off, he'd join like-minded reptile enthusiasts and academics on research projects, studying species like timber rattlesnakes in North America and king cobras in South Asia. Over these years, Nigel developed his method for radio-tracking snakes and now he's the go-to guy for any wildlife documentary involving snakes. He told me that his radio telemetry data shows clearly that adders in the UK are extremely faithful to specific areas. And that kind of information needs to be a vital consideration when it comes to wide-scale construction plans or mechanized habitat management, especially in the Midlands, where the number of adders is really low.

Adders are now considered an indicator species, which honours their vital role in an ecosystem. And as of 2022, Sites of Special Scientific Interest can now be nominated just to protect adders, which is a cool development. Unfortunately, no new sites have been announced, though. Part of the problem is that adders are already a kind of 'forgotten' species. In order to spread the word and the love for adders, people need to know about them and see them. This is why they're stuck in a Catch-22 situation, because if you broadcast the location of an adder site, a lot of people want to visit. And of course, the last thing you need around a load of adders is footfall! So it's vital to be secretive. Nigel smuggled me into one of his favourite adder sites in 2022. By the end of the day, we'd counted 43 adders. That's a testament to the hard work of volunteers undertaken over many years. Nigel told me that 43 was 'truly exceptional'. I told him he must be able to talk Parseltongue!

Nigel is one of the folks who take schoolkids (and the odd wildlife cameraman) out to safely see snakes in the wild. He made the very sensible point that the time to engage with kids about our native reptiles is when they're discovering how amazing dinosaurs were. And the way to do it is not just with a presentation or video, because, in Nigel's words, 'When kids actually see the thing, it changes everything. The first time you ever see a snake in the wild is an experience you won't forget. I never did and it's shaped my life.'

Nigel took the opportunity to very politely correct me that technically there aren't three snake species in the UK – there are four. A non-native snake has colonized two sites in the UK. It's the Aesculapian snake, which grows up to 2m (7ft) long, making it the largest of our snakes (and one of the largest in continental Europe, where it comes from). One of the populations is in Colwyn Bay in north Wales, just down the road from my beloved Bangor Uni (who have been studying them). It seems that they escaped from the Welsh Mountain Zoo in the 1970s. Aesculapian snakes are amazing tree climbers and aren't venomous or dangerous to humans. In fact, we should probably feel quite appreciative of them seeing as their favourite prey is the rat. You've probably seen an Aesculapian snake without knowing it – it's the snake that features on the famous medical symbol of a snake climbing a staff. And that's because the snake takes its name from Asclepius, the Greek god of medicine and healing. The other UK population of these beautiful olive, brown or grey snakes (which perform a completely mesmerizing mating 'dance') is in the centre of London! They're by Regent's Canal, right next to London Zoo. They didn't come from the zoo originally – it seems that they escaped from a local research facility. They've been here for 35 years, very happily catching rats, but very few people know about them. Until now, hopefully!

★ ★ ★

If I ask adults and kids to name me a snake in the UK, they almost always say 'adder', with a few mentioning the grass snake. But if I ask people to name a lizard, the room is a lot quieter. Some folks think it's a trick question, but we actually have three lizard species in the UK – the common lizard, the sand lizard and the slow worm. Confusingly, unlike the smooth snake, which is as you might expect both *smooth* and *a snake*, the slow worm is neither *slow* nor *a worm*. It looks like a snake, but it's not that either. It's a type of legless lizard. You can see how people get confused – a slow worm moves the same way as a snake and even has a tongue that it flicks in and out. The best way to tell them apart from a distance is the size – slow worms are usually about 30cm (12in) long whereas the smallest UK snake, the adder, is double that (and has a very distinctive thick black zig-zag pattern all the way down its back).

Male slow worms are brown or grey and females are more golden-brown with a thin dark line along their back. When you get a bit closer to a slow worm, you'll see that its head just looks like an extension of its body, a bit like they're just one long tube. A snake's head is wider and it has a slimmer neck region. Moving in even closer to a slow worm you'll see that it blinks – a snake doesn't have eyelids, so it can't do that. Also, a slow worm opens its mouth to stick its tongue out (which is nowhere near as deeply forked as a snake's tongue), whereas a snake's tongue just slips through a little gap while they keep their mouth closed. Slow worms are sometimes called blind worms, not because they're actually blind, but because their eyes are really tiny. It's only when you hold one that you realize how smooth they feel, and that's because their scales don't overlap. But you have to be really careful if you pick up a slow worm because if they feel threatened, they'll release a part of their tail. It's a clever way of being able to confuse a predator and get away, but it's the weirdest thing when you see that little section still wiggling away, completely detached from the rest of its body – it's like something out of a comedy horror film.

Amazingly, slow worms can live up to 30 years in the wild. They eat things like slugs, snails and beetles, so if you're a keen gardener, you'll be delighted to see a slow worm around. They mainly come out around dusk to hunt in grassland or in gardens, burrowing for grub. I used to strim the grass for a few of my neighbours in Ardnamurchan, and one particular house has a big compost heap at the back. I lifted some of the leaf mulch in the compost heap up to make room for the cut grass, and there were half a dozen slow worms as surprised to see me as I was to see them. But then I thought about it and it made perfect sense. Their food of choice is right there, attracted by the decaying leaf matter, and compost generates heat. So, for a cold-blooded reptile, it's a bit like having a lovely pub meal by the fire in winter!

Chapter 4

Farmland

———

We always had eggs for breakfast at home when I was a kid. And then one day at school, I found out about battery hens. The next day, before everyone woke up, I went downstairs and checked the back of the egg box. I couldn't find anything about battery hens, but I did find – in ridiculously small letters – the words 'produced by caged hens'. I appreciate that this now sounds like something you might find on 'Overheard in Waitrose', but that day, I said:

'Mama – I won't eat eggs that aren't free-range.'

My mum looked at my dad, puzzled.

'But eggs are your favourite breakfast, Hamza.'

I told her about the plight of battery hens, but she couldn't understand why this affected me so much, especially as, in Sudan, we'd left a country where people were literally starving.

'You should be thankful, Hamza!'

'I am thankful, mama, but I have to be respectful about the life of a chicken.'

Bless her – she spent part of that day learning all about caged hens and free-range hens. The next day, I found a different egg box on the counter. And on the box were the words 'Free Range'. My mum came downstairs and smiled at me. And she's never bought another egg from a battery hen.

Sometimes kids can be the engine room of change for their parents. And it's something that gives me a lot of hope. I love nothing more than seeing a family building a bug hotel together. Kids aren't going to remember the hours they spent watching cartoons, but they'll remember the time spent outdoors making something magical with their parents. I want more people to be the adult who encourages a young person outside and into the playground, the mud, the woods, the ponds, the rockpools. I heard a talk given at an educational event to a group of parents recently. It started with the question: 'Would you die for your kids?' Everyone nodded. He followed up with: 'Will you live for them?' It was a very powerful opening and it stayed with me. It reminded me of a phrase that I've carried with me for as long as I can remember: 'Live for Mother Nature, and in turn, Mother Nature will live for you.'

★ ★ ★

Farming is a hard profession, maybe even the hardest. I really feel for farmers. I know how hard they work, the incredibly long hours and the fact they often work 365 days a year. Farmers are incredibly self-sufficient and can fix anything – they're the ultimate can-do people. Usually, farmers descend from generations of farmers before them and I think most of them would tell you that it's harder to make money farming now than it's ever been. And that means farmers work even longer hours, often spending sustained periods of time alone and with the financial pressure of a very expensive outlay on machinery and equipment.

I've heard farmers say 'we've always done it this way', and much of the time, that works perfectly. Some things don't need to change. Using a sheepdog to herd sheep in a remote, mountainous part of Scotland is still the best way to do it. But some things can change. Instead of cutting hedges with a machine, you can partially cut their stems and bend them over onto their sides, so a year later they will still grow berries, which the waxwings and redwings eat in the wintertime. Hedges will help farmers grow stronger and more fertile soils and reduce the impact felt by direct rainfall. This kind of approach would benefit everyone.

Many farmers feel like they've got enough to worry about just to balance the books. Telling them they need to protect this animal or that plant is going to take some of their precious time and energy, I get that. And I get why someone not in the farming world who decides to pitch in and suggest how they could change things isn't going to be well received. It would be the same for me if a non-cameraperson started suggesting to me the best way to photograph an otter. I'd be more inclined to listen, though, to a cameraperson. Likewise, if the advice came from a fellow farmer, it might be a different matter. And, happily, because farming success stories with conservation in mind are becoming better known, more farmers might be inspired to follow their lead.

Farmers and conservationists have often found themselves on other sides of the farm fence. There's been the feeling that in order for conservation efforts to succeed on farmland, farmers have to make sacrifices. But times are changing. Sustainable farming has come along. The basic idea is to ensure that a farm is profitable, both financially and environmentally, so it can meet the needs of current and future generations. Twenty years ago, that idea probably would have sounded far-fetched or just impossible. Now it just sounds sensible.

The most important thing about sustainable farming is that it takes its lead from nature.

And that's a good call because nature has already solved many problems that human society faces. We've just chosen to ignore the solutions until recently. I'll give you an example that's dear to my heart. In the late 1970s, Japan's famous *shinkansen* (the bullet train) encountered a problem travelling through small, specially constructed tunnels. The fast-moving train compressed the air in front of it, creating a sound wave that came out of the other end of the tunnel like a gunshot. That sound disturbed the local wildlife, the local population and the passengers on the train. The compressed air was also slowing the train down. So engineers looked to nature for inspiration, which we now call 'biomimicry'. And they found it in the narrow, streamlined shape of a kingfisher's beak. When a kingfisher dives into the river for fish, its beak breaks the water at very high speed and makes only a tiny splash. So engineer (and birder) Eiji Nakatsu came up with the long, narrow, squashed-diamond-shaped locomotive. It reduced air resistance by 30 per cent, making the trains quicker and more efficient, and the gunshot was silenced.

When it comes to livestock grazing on farm fields, there is an alternative to piling on pesticides and fertilizers. We just needed to look to the migrating herds on the African savannahs. There, the wildebeest arrive and munch the grass, trample it, poo on the ground, then move to the next spot quickly. They don't want to stand around in their own dung. After they've moved on, the dung beetles turn up to tuck into their niche feast, and are soon followed by their predators, like egrets, secretary birds and mongooses. They're all moving after the large herds. A year later, the grazing herds have returned to the area they'd trampled. In that time, the broken-up ground has proved to be the perfect environment in which the grass seeds can grow, and it's come back stronger and thicker. Agitating the ground stimulates new life. You can see this in the New Forest, with the way that foxgloves spring up in the areas that have been disturbed by the wild ponies, cattle, donkeys or pigs.

There are also other benefits. Birds like cattle egrets hoover up the insects on and around the wildebeest so they're not suffering from flystrike in the way that farmed animals are. Flystrike is caused by flies laying their eggs in animals' fur, which hatch and turn into maggots, which then eat into the animals. I've seen it happen and it's bloody horrible. It can even be deadly.

Farmers can replicate the savannahs by allowing their cows to graze on a fenced-off area for a couple of days before moving them on to other pastures. Then the farmer moves the fence so the animals can graze in another area. It's a technique called rotational grazing or strip grazing. Then they open up the area that the cows had been on to the chickens, who'll scratch out all the manure and hoover up the bugs. Again, this follows exactly what happens on the African savannah. There are all sorts of benefits that come with this approach. Because the animals are moving quickly, young plant shoots aren't being stunted as a result of grazing taking place too early in their life cycles. The grass is able to recover and flourish, sending out all those sugars through their roots and into the soil.

And that creates stronger, healthier plants, which makes for higher-quality pasture.

Farms are typically family-run and have been in the same hands for generations. They're small communities that depend on each other, and in that sense, it's not a dissimilar set-up to village life in the Highlands. Things change slowly and, well, that's the way people like it. They need a little bit of convincing to embrace anything considered 'new-fangled', but it's worked for me in Ardnamurchan, whether it's encouraging friends and neighbours to leave areas of their garden wild or showing them footage of the spectacular creatures and scenery that you can capture perfectly with a drone. But there's a sense that the proof of the pudding is in the eating. And I think that applies to sustainable farming. It needs to show that it's working, and people need to see it with their own eyes to be convinced. Thanks to some absolute champions leading the way, it's doing that in spades.

This brings me on to an extraordinary farmer by the name of Patrick Barker. In 2005, Patrick and his cousin Brian took a bold leap. They saw a bright future for their 550-hectare family farm in mid-Suffolk, owned by their two fathers, and plucked up the courage to sit them down and tell them about the changes they'd implement to make the farm more efficient. As Patrick explained to me: 'We just went for it for a couple of hours and basically ran away afterwards leaving them to think it over.' I'm not sure anyone knew what to expect the following Monday morning, but as it happened, their dads came into the office and said, 'We like what you've come up with. Let's run with it.'

Patrick and Brian got cracking that second. The game-changer was the government's Higher Level Stewardship (HLS) scheme, launched in 2008. 'That was an epiphany to us,' Patrick explained. The scheme rewards farmers for environmentally focused management practices. As Patrick told me, they saw it as a way of taking out all the bits of the farm that weren't productive or efficient. So they planted flowers over the area where the pond was filled in 1970. They stopped trying to farm in triangle-shaped fields, took all the corners out and started farming in straight lines. They mapped out every single habitat on the farm and connected them all together with hedges and grass margins. They started to create a landscape. At the centre of the farm was a really long, thin 8.5-acre field with water courses on both sides, footpaths and a telegraph pole in the middle. Brian said, 'This is the heart of the farm. This should be a whole grassland corridor.' So they created wildflower meadows, but as with everything Patrick and Brian do, they really thought about it. Rather than buying an off-the-shelf seed mix, they went to their local village green which is a county wildlife site as a species-rich wildflower meadow. They cut the hay and baled it up. As the hay dried out, the seeds dropped down. As Patrick explained: 'We had a seed source that was absolutely bespoke to this area. All of a sudden, the heart of the farm was flowers and insects.'

The HLS scheme had identified the grey partridge as one of its target species. It's an umbrella species, which means that if we create the right habitat to support it, all sorts of other species will benefit. Patrick and Brian saw results very soon. 'Not only were there three or four pairs of grey partridges, there were yellowhammers, chaffinches and linnets everywhere,' Patrick told me.

Patrick met with Steve Piotrowski, the bird author and farmland wildlife advisor who was leading the Suffolk Community Barn Owl Project. Patrick invited him to put some barn owl boxes up. While they didn't get barn owls straight away, the following summer, Patrick discovered a brood of kestrel chicks inside one of the boxes. 'That was a huge moment for me,' Patrick told me. Steve also showed Patrick how he rang the chicks, and I know very well how transformative that moment can be. You appreciate them on a deeper level – you realize quite how extraordinary their anatomy is, how light they are and how quickly their hearts beat. Patrick discovered all of that, but with an added dimension, as he told me: 'Bird-ringing also gave me a way of quantifying success, which is so important to me. That experience lit a fire under me and I started training to be a bird-ringer.' Yes, Patrick!

They mapped out a two-year hedge-planting plan to add to the existing ancient hedgerows. They now have 48km (30 miles) of hedgerow on their farm, all geared towards supporting as many species as possible. 'That was a theme that was working through all the habitats: how do we get all these habitats working as hard as we possibly can?' Patrick told me. So into their new hedges, they added buckthorn, privet and holly – flowering species that provided a nectar source and a fruit source for animals. With all that grub, Patrick knew they'd attract more birds, who would breed earlier and be in better shape, so they'd be more likely to have three broods instead of two for the year. That would be a huge biodiversity win.

'Farmers have always focused on yield; I think it's all about margin. I value yield in a different way. In every habitat on the farm, I want a yield of wildlife,' Patrick told me. I feel like someone should make a film about Patrick and Brian's farm. It's been an inspiring, incredible journey for them. What they've created, over the past 20 years, is a farm with nature in mind, run by a pair of conservationist farmers. But it's also a sustainable and profitable farm, and it's inspired other farmers to do things differently. Their hard work led to the Silver Lapwing Award in 2009 – 'the Champions League of landscape farming conservation', as Patrick put it. They also won Countryside Farmer of the Year at the 2010 Farmers Weekly Awards.

The Barkers opened their farm up to the public, hosting visits from fellow farmers, history groups and the Women's Institute as well as hundreds of schoolchildren. The farm even became part of their local primary school's programme of outdoor learning experiences. It is now a platform for knowledge exchange across the wider farming world. The Barkers are always analysing the impact and effectiveness of everything they're doing. If it doesn't work as well as they want, they tinker. They are constantly evolving, and this makes it such an exciting place to visit.

Patrick told me that he has recorded 727 species on their farm (including flowers), but by the time this book's come out, that might be a few more! They have 58 species of bee, including *Melitta tricincta* (the red bartsia bee), which has only been recorded in Suffolk four times. They now have great crested newts in the ponds they've restored. Patrick runs moth traps and has recorded 470 species of moth on their farm. In late 2024, they found a species of ant (*Stenamma westwoodii*) that's only been recorded in Suffolk twice and in the UK 32 times. They found it because no one had thought to go and look in the composty layer of winter cover crops for a solitary species of ant before. 'All the ant people are thrilled about it!' Patrick told me, excitedly, before adding: 'And it all gives me more incentive to research what it needs to help it thrive now that it's found a home on the farm.'

As a testament to the success of what Patrick and his cousin have initiated, they're getting approached by some of the biggest companies in the world, who are keen to find out how they can be successful from a financial and biodiversity and sustainability standpoint.

Patrick and Brian have combined ancient stewardship techniques with the best of modern technology. Nature hasn't been an afterthought – it's been key to their success. The farm's making money, it's much kinder to the environment and it's become a biodiversity haven. Everything feels like it's in a state of harmonious balance. Look after Mother Nature and Mother Nature will look after you.

I could see what was different about Patrick's farm as soon as I set foot on his land. There are bees, butterflies, hoverflies and dragonflies everywhere, buzzing and beavering away. It feels like somewhere between a farm and a nature reserve. Patrick and Brian ensure that the vegetation in their fields is always a range of heights, densities and ages to provide cover and sustenance for different birds, bugs, bats and small mammals. The spiders, beetles and hoverflies are attracted to the flowering margins, and they're feasting on the aphids trying to munch on the crops. I can see why they don't need insecticides. And then, darting across a field, I saw a brown hare, which always gets me really excited. When I last visited Patrick, the whole farm was hoaching full of hares. Patrick told me that through his nightscope, they count between 20 and 30 brown hares. We're not talking about across the whole farm – we're talking per field. It's like every hare in the UK has been teleported onto their farm. A big reason for that is because of their crop rotation. It means that unlike the historic cereal-growing landscape of the region, which is basically brown stubble by September, the Barkers have green cover throughout the year.

Brown hares are magnificent creatures. The agility and power they have in those back legs are astonishing. A brown hare in full flight mode is an extraordinary thing. It's our fastest land mammal, reaching speeds of 70kph (45mph) so nothing's catching it in the wild. It's a lot bigger than a rabbit, reaching up to 70cm (28in) long and weighing up to 5kg (11lb), which just for reference is about the same as a small Jack Russell. Rabbits rarely grow past 40cm (16in) and they top out weight-wise at 2kg (4½lb). Hares are more rusty-brown, whereas rabbits are grey-brown, and hares' ears are quite a bit longer and with black tips. But it looks more or less like a turbocharged rabbit.

Some of the best acrobatics I've ever seen is by a brown hare escaping an eagle. They strafe in a zig-zag pattern and then suddenly leap up, with perfect timing, so that the eagle swoops in underneath them and misses. It reminds me of that scene in *Top Gun* when Tom Cruise hits the brakes, pulls up hard and says, 'He'll fly right by!' of the enemy jet pursuing him. I can't imagine what's going on in the eagle's brain when a hare pulls out that move. WTF!

Farmland has changed quite a bit since the 19th century, and that's been problematic for hares. There used to be more of a mixture of fields – grass, cereals, winter cereals and root crops. Farms tend to be more specialized now, and many fields have been enlarged, which means hares have to keep moving to find the best grazing. Fewer fields are fallow and grass and meadows are cut more often, so that doesn't help hares either. Put all this together and it's no wonder that hares are just about surviving rather than thriving. But there are things farmers can do without making too much of a sacrifice. The first thing is to cut fields from the centre rather than from the outside in, which gives hares a good chance to escape the mower. Even better is to leave unmowed and unfertilized areas in field corners so baby hares (leverets) can hide there. Their best defence is to remain hidden. Without that cover, leverets are going to be easy pickings for a hungry fox.

In mating season, hares' behaviour completely changes. Usually they're elusive, solitary and secretive sorts, but they become really lively. This ends up in what is often described as 'boxing', squaring up to each other and standing on their back legs, frantically waving their front legs about trying to punch each other in the face. It's somewhere between Victorian fisticuffs and squabbling toddlers and is quite extraordinary to watch. And unusually for animals, it's not two males going toe to toe – it's a female standing up to a randy male, who's probably been chasing her for over an hour, and she's decided she's had enough! This behaviour is where the expression 'mad as a March hare' comes from.

Unlike rabbits, who build warrens underground to raise their young, hares live out in the open. They dig shallow trenches called 'forms' in which they lie completely still with their ears pinned back, almost entirely concealed below ground. Forms are higher at the back than at the front, so the hares can push off as fast as possible when danger approaches, like Olympic sprinters exploding out of their starting blocks. They also position their form in a vantage point over the surrounding land and angle them to face downhill, so that gravity can assist them when they bolt. Hares are clever, you see – they plan their escape in advance. When they're a little spooked and want a peek at what's going on around, they lift their head slightly like a periscope before popping back down again.

The green cover, the hedges, the fallow land and the wildflowers are all such valuable habitats. When I visited Patrick and Brian's farm, I saw yellowhammers, grey partridges and turtle doves, which is a rare privilege. Turtle doves have been on the UK's Red List (the birds most at risk of local extinction) since it was first published in 1996. There are thought to be only 3,600 turtle dove territories across the whole of the UK, and having such beautiful creatures on your farm is an honour. Their chestnut, chessboard-pattern wing feathers and black and white neck stripes look like they've been painted by an artist or made by a bespoke tailor. And their gentle, purring, cooing song makes older folks reminisce wistfully about the 'sound of summers gone by', while younger folks compare it to ASMR. It's reassuring, soothing and uplifting, somehow making you feel like everything's right with the world.

Patrick and Brian extend an open invitation to biology and conservation students to use the farm for their research. Patrick's take is that he and Brian manage the landscape, and students are welcome to observe and record the effects. It feels like the Barkers have literally brought the outside world in. Nature's part of the team here. They even invited all the neighbouring farmers to see what they'd been up to and how it all works, and they had a great response. So Patrick and Brian formed the High Suffolk Farm Cluster, which comprises 14 local farms working together both to manage the landscape more collaboratively and to farm better and more sustainably. Now that so many of the neighbouring farmers have been inspired by Patrick's example, the Barkers' farm is no longer just a lone green oasis anymore. The green veins are coursing through the countryside again, bringing an ecosystem back to life.

Chapter 5

Woodland

———

If I told you that north Wales was home to one of the most beautiful rainforests in the world, you'd wonder if I'd taken a wrong turn down the M6. But we do have rainforests in the UK, just maybe not the type you might be imagining. You see, there are two types of rainforest: tropical and temperate. Temperate rainforests used to cover huge areas of the British Isles, but only clumps remain near the west coast. In the UK, the temperate rainforest is known as Atlantic rainforest or Atlantic woodland, and incredibly, it's probably even more threatened than tropical rainforest.

The best way to describe Atlantic rainforest is that you feel like you've entered an enchanted land. It's completely different from the habitat you will have just walked through to get there. Usually, these forests are hidden away in gorges and there's a river running through them. The air feels different as you approach – it's humid, and the temperature feels a little milder. And then, suddenly, everything around you is carpeted in rich, luscious greens of every possible shade. There are probably small boulders and tree roots and stumps, all of which are covered in moss, liverworts and incredible species of lichen. Every single surface feels full of life. There's a moment in the Disney film *Moana*, right towards the end, where the goddess Te Fiti touches the ground, and plants start springing up absolutely everywhere. That's what it's like in a temperate rainforest. There are trees that you might never have seen together, with sessile oaks nestled next to willows, rowans, hazels and birches. It's utterly extraordinary.

I was talking to a friend about the temperate rainforest, and it became a lightbulb moment for him. He told me that he and his wife got lost in Dartmoor and found this completely extraordinary landscape by a river that looked like the Shire in *The Lord of the Rings*. 'That's it, my friend. You've found Atlantic rainforest!' I told him. He said they'd tried to return several times but never found it. Fortunately, the clever folks who run the Lost Rainforests of Britain campaign put together an interactive map in 2022 that shows you exactly where the remaining fragments are. They're concentrated along the coasts of western Britain in what's known as the hyper-oceanic zone. Western Scotland has the largest area, followed by the Lake District, north Wales, south-east Wales and Dartmoor, but you also find pockets inland along river gorges.

It was my favourite botanist and former lecturer Nigel Brown who first showed me Atlantic rainforest, in north Wales. 'Ah yes – I remember!' he told me when we chatted on the phone. 'All the 50 shades of green that it produces is something that everyone should behold at least once in their lives,' he said in typically poetic fashion. Nigel also told me a bit more about the specific requirements of Atlantic rainforest: a minimum of around 1,400mm (55in) of rain, about 180 wet days a year, a mean winter temperature no lower than 2°C (36°F) and a summer maximum of approximately 19°C (66°F). The humid, mild conditions are ideal for around 200 species of lichen and the same number of mosses, liverworts and hornworts. There are also probably 30 species of fern, including some of our rarest, like Killarney fern and the filmy ferns, which are mainly warm, temperate or tropical species. 'You feel as if you're walking into a habitat that's out of place latitude-wise,' Nigel said. 'In a sense, you're also looking back in time to a habitat that used to be much more widespread.'

Lichen doesn't get a lot of love, but it should. Lichen absorbs water straight from the atmosphere, and is especially sensitive to the air quality, which makes it a very useful bioindicator. Lichen comes in so many shapes, sizes and colours, and over 85 per cent of the UK's 1,500 species of lichen are in Scotland. As Nigel explained, this is part of what gives Atlantic rainforest its textural variety. The fruticose lichens form these incredible hanging pendant shapes. One of my favourites is known as 'old man's beard', and it's the perfect description, because it's bushy, messy, dangly and kind of has a life of its own!

There's also the lush-looking evergreen lungwort, which 'almost look like a direct connection with seaweeds and the sea' to borrow Nigel's beautiful words. And then there are the mosses, which form so many different surfaces and patterns. Nigel told me that the beautiful pincushion-like mosses, such as *Leucobryum*, are actually so hard you could sit on them and leave no impression. His favourite time to walk through the Atlantic rainforest in

Wales is in the winter, because the lack of canopy means more light reaches the ground. 'That's when you can really see the greenness of the mosses and lichens, as well as the evergreen ferns.' He loves sphagnum moss, a key component of Atlantic rainforest. And to be fair, it does get easily overlooked, until your lecturer invites you to have a look at it under a microscope. It was blindingly beautiful. 'It looks like this most wonderfully elaborate lattice and mosaic of green cells suspended in a series of bubble-like containers, but it's the way they hang everything else together which is so captivating,' Nigel told me, with the kind of passionate flourish that brought the plant world to life for a lecture theatre full of 20-year-olds. In Chapter 2, I listed my big five nature heroes: David Attenborough, Steve Irwin, Jane Goodall, Dian Fossey and Peter Scott. Nigel Brown is, without a doubt, number six.

Atlantic rainforest is a type of ancient wood, which means it has to have existed continuously since 1600 in England, Wales and Northern Ireland or since 1750 in Scotland. Ancient woods are so important to us because they've been largely undisturbed, and that means a unique community of fungi, plants, insects, birds and mammals coexist there and have done for centuries. Sadly, only

2.5 per cent of the UK is covered by ancient woodland, but in places, that figure is rising. There's one in Northern Ireland that I really love, and it's open to the public for the first time in 500 years. In 2021, the Woodland Trust bought 156 hectares of the Mourne Park estate in County Down, including 73 hectares of ancient woodland. So much work has gone on to clear invasive species like rhododendrons. I know their flowers are beautiful, but they grow super quickly and crowd out other plants as well as often carrying a disease fatal to over 150 plant species.

Woodland cover in Northern Ireland is the lowest of any part of Europe, at only 8.7 per cent, and ancient woodland accounts for just 0.04 per cent of the Northern Irish landscape. The great news is that the Woodland Trust has bought another 32 hectares of neighbouring land thanks to a tremendous joint funding effort from Ulster Garden Villages (a charity committed to improving the lives of people in Northern Ireland), the government and private donations. Everyone's come together because it's a cause that unites everyone. It's nature's treasure chest. No one wants to see ancient woodland and treasured native species disappear, do they?

★ ★ ★

The larch has a special place in my heart. It's the tree that my beloved white-tailed eagles hang about in on the west coast of Scotland – and if it's good enough for them, it's good enough for me!

The larch is an unusual tree because it's a conifer but it's not evergreen. I know what you might be thinking – all conifers are evergreens, right? Almost all of them. Out of the over 600 species of conifer, 20 of them are deciduous. And that means that the larch goes from that fresh, vibrant green that's full of the joys of spring to blue-green and finally gold in autumn, when they decide that it's time to shed their needle-like leaves. They leave a golden carpet beneath the tree, which is made even more spectacular by the fact that larches often stand alone in Scotland, in stunning, inaccessible locations. And there's good reason for that, which I'll get on to. Their pinecones don't fall with the needles, though – they remain on the tree, sometimes for many years, eventually turning grey-black. That's an easy way to tell them apart from other trees in winter. Look for the upright cones and the big buds.

As much as I love the larch and its golden leaves, for me, the gold medal has to go to the Scots pine. Somehow, pines have a bad rep. When you say 'pine', most people think of cheap furniture. They also tend to think of pine plantations – evenly spaced rows of trees that ultimately become timber. The Scots pine is a different beast. It's Britain's only native pine tree and we're right at the western edge of its global range. Scots pines form part of the ancient Caledonian Forest (Caledonia being the name the Romans came up with for Scotland), which in turn is part of the boreal forest – the mostly coniferous forests growing in high-latitude environments, or what I like to call the dark-green headband near the top of the world.

I'd seen pockets of Caledonian Forest across the Highlands, but it was when I travelled to Glen Tanar, a national nature reserve in the Cairngorms, to film *Wild Isles* in 2022, that I *got* it. It was the largest expanse of Caledonian Forest I'd been to, and it was almost like I'd entered some kind of religious ceremony. You're in awe of the age, grace, beauty and stillness in front of you, and you can't help but wonder why we've chopped any of it down. Ferns and heather in the understorey at Glen Tanar grow all the way up to your chest, providing the perfect cover for birds and deer. That scrubby area of vegetation between grassland or farmland and woodland is so important. It doesn't get much love because it's an in-between place and it doesn't look like much, but that's often where the most magic happens. There are more species inhabiting the first 10m (33ft) of any woodland edge than inhabit the remainder of the woodland beyond it. That scrubby area, that no one seems to really value, is a kind of convergence zone, similar to the intertidal region, the great meeting place between land and sea.

Glen Tanar feels like it hasn't been touched by humankind, and it has deepened my belief that Scotland is the most beautiful place on earth. Glen Tanar is one of the 35 remnants (spanning a total of 20,000 hectares) of Caledonian Forest dotted across the Highlands. And every Scots pine you see there is a direct descendant of the first Scots pines that established themselves in Britain, about 9,600 years ago. In those little havens, you'll find some of Britain's most remarkable creatures, including pine martens, red squirrels, the Scottish wildcat, capercaillies and golden eagles. Creatures that I desperately hope will not pass into myth and legend like the animals that roamed this exact spot 7,000 years ago. Back then, you would have found brown bears, grey wolves, wild boar, elk, beavers and wild horses. And the forest wouldn't have been confined to green Highland islands. It would have stretched across 1.5 million hectares, from the Atlantic to the North Sea. It would have been one enormous enchanted forest.

At Glen Tanar, the older pines are known locally as granny trees or nanny trees and some of them are over 700 years old. They're grizzled, gnarly survivors. What's incredible is seeing these trees marked on ancient maps, then you walk around the estate and see the very same tree, with the extraordinary added bonus that it now contains a golden eagle nest and little eaglets. Golden eagles like older Scots pines that are tall and broad, kind of like an amphitheatre. There are also goshawks, who like close-together juvenile Scots pines that are tall and straight and haven't been coppiced. Goshawks need this kind of specific habitat because they want to feel protected nesting high up in the trees (although the only predator in the UK that would cause them any trouble is a spectacularly brave pine marten on the hunt for eggs) and also need to be able to manoeuvre through the trees unseen to ambush birds and small mammals. Goshawks are sometimes called the phantoms of the forest because they ambush their prey silently, barely beating their wings when they swoop down from their roost, reaching speeds of up to 40kph (25mph) and using their big rudder of a tail to make sharp turns. When I first saw one, the thought that came into my head was: 'Wow, they're like sparrowhawks on steroids!' And if you've ever seen a sparrowhawk and a goshawk side by side, it's like you're looking at featherweight fighter next to a heavyweight.

When I'm walking through a wood in Scotland and I hear the call of a goshawk, I'm excited, not just because there's a chance of seeing one, but because it tells me that there is a healthy ecosystem here that can sustain it. It means there are probably thriving red squirrel, pine marten and songbird populations. Goshawks will make themselves at home in a quiet and fairly dense part of a wood. They're not like red kites or buzzards who are perfectly happy in open areas. Goshawks are more discerning house-hunters. They don't want a mature, super bushy big tree. And they don't want a young, flimsy tree. Their nests are quite substantial and they like to place them where the trunk starts branching out, so if I was an avian estate agent, I'd point them in the direction of an 80-year-old Scots pine. It's a high-class tree for a high-class hawk. A goshawk knows what it wants and if it doesn't get it, it's taking its business elsewhere! They want to be in a place that favours the (to quote Liam Neeson from the film *Taken*) 'very particular set of skills' they possess that makes them a nightmare for their prey: aerobatic agility in a confined woodland setting.

Goshawks spend hours, completely motionless, monitoring everything around them. And then once something has flown into their layer, they pursue it like a stealth fighter jet. Their musculature means that they turn the burners on so quickly that the prey usually doesn't know what's coming until it's being snatched out of the air. Not only can goshawks practically dislocate their shoulders to fit through tight spaces – transforming into a torpedo – but they also repurpose their broad tail as a third wing to give them extra lift when they need it. When you've held a goshawk and you truly get a sense of their sheer power and size, it doesn't seem possible. They're a kind of contortionist assassin, armed with a complete mental picture of their environment. They know the swiftest route through the trees, and like a sparrowhawk, they've rehearsed it many times.

The best chance you have of seeing a goshawk is on a still early spring morning, when they briefly abandon their woodland homes to court each other in the open sky. You might hear them in a forest, especially when their white, fluffy chicks are young. I used to ring them in north Wales with my friend Tony Cross and I remember their beautiful grey eyes. Goshawks are notoriously hard to film – in fact, it's probably harder to film a goshawk than a golden eagle, and that's saying something. Golden eagles require patience, preparation and silence but the location of a goshawk's nest in dense woodland means that you've got to somehow assemble a camera in a neighbouring tree that gives you a clear view. You have to either get lucky or spend some time pruning suitable trees in the hope that a goshawk will select it, which they never do! White-tailed eagles are much more considerate!

★ ★ ★

Just 30 miles east from Glen Tanar along the beautiful River Dee is another part of this enchanted forest: Mar Lodge, in the heart of the Cairngorms, and it's a wonderful woodland success story. At nearly 30,000 hectares, it's the largest national nature reserve in the UK and the location couldn't be more breathtaking. The story began over 25 years ago, when the National Trust for Scotland (NTS) made the difficult decision to cull the population of red deer. No one goes into conservation wanting to see animals killed, but at that time, there didn't seem to be another choice. The land simply couldn't support those numbers of red deer and this was the only way to give the trees and plants a chance to survive and restore balance to the ecosystem.

It was far from an overnight success but it always takes longer to repair something than to destroy it. Several years later, the Scots pines were regenerating but slowly. They just needed more time to get going. An independent review commissioned by the NTS in 2011 led to a 4.7-km (2.9-mile) fence being erected along a small section of the estate's southern border (close to the lodge itself), which helped, but it was the continued management of the deer population that started to achieve results. By 2015, some of the Scots pine saplings had doubled in size. In 2016, a survey revealed that 835 hectares of pine forest were regenerating. In 2017, Mar Lodge was declared a national nature reserve and in 2021, the naturally regenerating pine forest covered an incredible 1,972 hectares.

Once Mother Nature has what she needs, it's incredible how quickly she can flourish. The impact went way beyond the Scots pine trees, and this is one of the most exciting possibilities of conservation projects. You often start off intending to save a single species. But that species is intimately interconnected with dozens of others. It's not just the Scots pines that were no longer being nibbled by the deer. Birches, willows and juniper trees were growing taller and looking healthier. Little aspen saplings began to rise above the heather, which had botanists scratching their heads. Aspens are one of Britain's most beautiful trees. They're stunning deciduous hardwood trees closely related to poplars and willows that turn bright-yellow in autumn. Aspens have rounded leaves with little blunt 'teeth' along the margins and are attached to a long stalk, so they flutter even when you can't really feel any wind. That's what earned them the scientific name *tremula* and its nickname 'quaking aspen'. Rather wonderfully, I've heard them called 'the tremlin tree' in the Highlands, which sounds so poetic in a Scottish voice.

Unfortunately for aspens, they've also managed that rarest of combinations: they're both highly nutritious and really tasty. Deer love to chomp on them, so the ones that have survived are in the few places that even deer can't get to. That's why you might see a lonely golden-yellow aspen on a rocky crag overlooking a stream.

The prevailing wisdom was that aspens very rarely release seeds in Scotland. It could be because the cool, oceanic climate means that they only tend to flower in a hot dry summer, the last of which was in 2019. And the last time before that was in the late 1990s. It could also have something to do with the fertility of aspen trees decreasing over time. Getting aspens to set seed is a problem across the UK in general. But in 2017, a chap called Robert Lee, the director of the tree seed supplier Forestart, came up with an idea. He simulated a beaver attack by removing an inch-wide ring of bark (not all the way around, which would kill the tree) from a number of aspen trees. Eight of the aspens reacted to the shock by flowering, as Robert had predicted. And the trees all healed well. This could be a game-changer for aspens in Scotland.

As it is, aspens have another method of reproduction. They rely on their impressive root system that sends up shoots known as 'suckers' to create clones of themselves. Eventually, these clones can grow roots of their own and become independent of the parent tree. But sometimes you can have a whole grove of what look like separate aspens that are actually still all the same tree! The world's largest tree is an aspen that includes 47,000 clones connected by a single 106-acre root system. It's known as *Pando*, which is Latin for 'I spread', and has been labelled one of the

40 Wonders of America. It's thought to weigh 6,000t, also making it the heaviest organism in the world. This will come in very handy at a pub quiz!

But in Mar Lodge, little aspen saplings were appearing many hundreds of metres away from other mature aspens – well beyond the reach of their root system. There were only two possible explanations, both of which would have been big news. Either the mature aspens had been secretly flowering and releasing seeds, or, despite being constantly munched, the little ones had been surviving beneath other vegetation. That makes sense – their root systems can live underground for over 100 years waiting for the right time to send those suckers northwards again up through the soil. They are tough trees. They're also one of our oldest native trees, taking a foothold in Scotland 2,000 years earlier than Scots pines. Like the oak, aspens are a keystone species – they're the glue that holds a habitat together. Four UK species rely on the aspen, including the aspen hoverfly and the dark bordered beauty moth (what a name that is!). Around 300 types of lichen and 266 types of fungi have been recorded on Scottish aspens. Aspens also exist happily by rivers and streams, which means their roots provide shelter for fish, and their leaves attract insects, which the fish will eat. Their leaves enrich the watercourses and the soil. Aspens also grow and spread quickly, which makes them especially good at storing carbon. All in all, the aspen is a biodiversity magnet and a biological wonder.

The regeneration of the aspens was an offshoot of the Scots pine success. And it wasn't the only one. Many species of orchid were reappearing in parts of the estate where they'd never been seen. Heather and wildflowers were filling the land with colour and the grateful buzzing of insects. It goes to show if you give Mother Nature a helping hand then the whole landscape will benefit. It's a bit like making someone's day with a random act of kindness. The positive impact of that gesture can go beyond anything you ever thought possible. The joy that you spread is likely to rub off, even just a little bit, on people that they know and interact with. It's not only the landscape that will benefit. It's you and me. Mar Lodge is a pioneering project to be proud of that attracts international interest and encourages other similar projects around the world. If our native biodiversity returns, people want to visit. If you commercialize it in the right way, with camping, glamping, a sustainable produce shop and 'wildlife safaris', you can create a successful business.

I was lucky enough to visit the site and meet the inspirational people behind the scenes. It was a real privilege. One of them is the incredible Shaila Rao, the conservation manager at the estate. When Shaila first came to Mar Lodge, over 20 years ago, she was studying mountain hares for her PhD. She fell in love with the landscape but noticed that the woodland was in pretty poor condition. She told me she also wondered how incredible this landscape could be if it was restored to its rightful glory. So when an ecologist job came up at Mar Lodge, she leaped at it – as did her husband in fact, but Shaila pipped him to the post!

When Shaila started her job, she noticed that the vegetation around the spectacular granny trees was cropped really short and there were no young trees coming through. 'Overgrazing meant that the woodland hadn't naturally regenerated in the last 200 to 300 years. So what we were looking at was a dying forest,' she told me. That's what they've been seeking to remedy at Mar Lodge. After considering all sorts of measures, like extensive fencing, the National Trust for Scotland, who own Mar Lodge, made the tough decision to reduce the number of deer. This decision was hugely unpopular among both the surrounding sporting estates and the local community who felt that it would seriously impact tourism. And, as Shaila told me, it wasn't like they were able to point to the regenerating woodland because it took some time for that to happen. 'But as soon as the trees started to appear above the heather, then people's opinions changed,' she told me. 'It was becoming a recovering, healthy forest again before their eyes.' Finally, they could see the impact that overgrazing had caused. More and more tourists wanted to see what was happening up at Mar Lodge. Let the landscape regenerate and people will come!

I remember coming up and seeing the golden eagles at Mar Lodge, and Shaila's friend and colleague Euan Weston showed me what he called a 'double-decker nest' – two nests on the same tree on top of each other – it was utterly incredible. The knock-on effect of the reduced grazing pressure and the regenerating woodland is better nesting habitats for birds, including one of our rarest birds of prey in the UK: the hen harrier. Now that the grasslands aren't being cropped so short, all the little voles, field mice and dormice are able to thrive, and with that food source, birds of prey will move in. Shaila told me that, in 2023, 8 of their 11 hen harrier pairs fledged chicks and that a grand total of 32 of them were born that year. When you consider that there are only around 650 hen harrier pairs in the whole of the UK, that is absolutely stunning. And Shaila has high hopes for the crested tit, which at the moment can only be found in ancient Caledonian Forest and Scots pine plantations 70–80km (40–50 miles) north of the Cairngorms. 'If it could make its way here through the corridors of woodland we're creating, that would be such a victory in terms of habitat connectivity.' Shaila and the team at Mar Lodge are creating the green veins through which biodiversity can flow. It's a beautiful thought and an inspiration to us all.

Chapter 6

Meadows and Moorland

———

Wildflower meadows have to be the loudest, most colourful and most joyful habitat we have. It's like a mini carnival among the grassland. But it's more than a floral display: a single meadow can contain 3 million wildflowers belonging to over 100 different species. And where you've got wildflowers, the bees, butterflies and birds will follow. Meadows are like a biodiversity engine room. And some of the most amazing examples are in Northumberland National Park.

In July, the Northumberland hay meadows are full of bright-yellow and purple flowers, providing an incredible colour contrast. Many of the flowers are really striking, like melancholy thistles, named so because they were once used to treat 'melancholia', or what we now call depression. They're unusual for a thistle because they don't have any spines, they grow over 1m (3ft) tall and look spectacular, like something out of the Chelsea Flower Show. Wood cranesbill is a bright-violet geranium and although it looks very pretty in flower, to a birder like me it looks even better after the flower head has fallen away – because that's when the remarkable crane's head shape appears that earns the cranesbill its name. Then, in the yellow corner, you've got yellow rattle, with its tube-like flowers. And again, when the flower fades, the show's not over, because that's when its dry seed pods rattle in the wind. It's also a really special plant because it helps to create flower-rich meadows. And that's because its roots attach to nearby grasses, which weakens the grass and allows other wildflowers to establish themselves. You might even find the northern marsh orchid, with its pinky-purple flowers, the lesser butterfly orchid and the remarkable bee orchid. That's one of the things I love about hay meadows – you never know which species have colonized it.

Meadows look breathtaking when they stretch across slopes into the distance, but anyone with a garden can have a little meadow if they set aside an area. They function like little service stations for pollinators. And they work really well when you add a tree or a bramble bush into the landscape, because that way, you'll further increase the biodiversity. I don't use any insecticides or pesticides in my garden so I've got hundreds of slugs and snails, which the mama song thrush is especially grateful for. In fact, she was so happy that she and her partner built their nest in the hedge that I planted a few years ago and raised their two chicks. I left the brambles in front of the hedge to grow (I can't claim this was a deliberate act – I actually meant to cut it back but I was lazy and forgot), but it turned out that the thrushes loved this feature, because it gave them extra cover and protection, plus a lovely supply of juicy berries, right on their doorstep. I've got goldfinches foraging naturally, sitting on a long stem and eating the seeds out of a thistle. That's what they'd been doing for thousands of years before we turned up. It makes me wonder what would happen if we could scale my garden up to the size of a football pitch – just think about the amount of wildlife that would appear. The best thing you can do for a meadow is to remember to cut it after the middle of July. That way, the wildflowers are able to set seed, so they'll grow again next year.

I was washing up the dishes in my sink, overlooking the garden, when suddenly I heard some serious rustling by the brambles. My first thought was that I'd attracted rats into the garden, but then I saw that snuffly snout and I knew it was a hedgehog. Leaving the brambles to grow was a happy accident – a family of hedgehogs had decided it was the perfect home for them. What I've learned is that sometimes, doing very little to a landscape is the best way for nature to thrive. It's not a great catchphrase though, 'I'm doing nothing to help the planet', so let's call it 'active inaction' because you do need to stay on top of it. A friend in Brighton told me recently that the council go around spraying weeds where people's front gardens meet the road with weedkiller. Sometimes weeds might not look pretty (some do, though!), but those flowers are just as helpful for birds, bees, wasps, butterflies and bats as flowers you've planted.

Jeff and Sandra, who live near me, have about an acre in front of their house and they've let it grow wild too except for a zig-zag path up to the house that's kept very neatly. That way, the wild section looks intentional. I understand it – many people worry about what their friends and neighbours are going to think. Luckily for me, I don't mind. Nature can do whatever it likes at my place as long as I can see out of my windows and the roof's still on. If you want to see birds, bees or butterflies in your garden, you're going to need to offer them a food source and shelter.

I used to go around the village mowing people's lawns, but I slowly converted my friends and neighbours to my way of thinking and they're all seeing the benefits. Granted, I did myself out of a job, but now the whole place is alive with nature. It isn't just one refuge that birds, bats and insects can visit. There's lots to go around. Once a year, at the end of autumn, it's safe to cut everything back – or do what I do and wait for the local sheep to stroll into my garden. Sheep are effectively nature's lawnmowers and their local owners are quite happy to let them wander far and wide. Once I see that they're in my garden and very happily munching away, I close the gate. Two days later, they've cleared the back garden and I can tell when they're done because I've got three faces staring at me through the window asking me, 'Where's the grub at?' Then I open the gate and they wander into next door's garden.

I know some people don't want to leave their grass to grow wild. I get it – having a neat, perfectly rectangular lawn looks lovely and there's something uniquely British about it. But I think there's a way that you can have both a lovely lawn and something even lovelier – a little wildlife sanctuary with all the chirping, buzzing and fluttering that it brings. My neighbour, Gail, asked me if I could strim the rough area under the trees in her garden, and I suggested leaving it to grow, seeing as no one walks that way anyway. She was worried it might look a bit messy. 'Not if you make it look like you've intended it,' I said. So we agreed that I'd mow the main lawn and leave the bits around the trees as a standing feature. Two years later, a pair of common sandpipers from the bay walked the 30m (100ft) from the edge of the loch and discovered Gail's garden and decided that the area of rough grass was the perfect place to raise their family. Now, Gail calls me up excitedly to tell me that the sandpipers are sitting on her wall. She's completely invested in their welfare, which is wonderful, and she now goes around telling people to let areas of their garden grow wild. My Scottish mother and father, Amanda and Chris, have a neat lawn in the back garden, but they've let their front garden grow wild either side of the path. Now, elephant hawk moths feed on the wildflowers at dusk. Jackpot!

This is the best part of making an effort to attract wildlife to your garden – the moment when a plant appears unexpectedly or when a creature you've been hoping for pays you a visit and decides that the accommodation and grub are to their liking. I wear it with pride, like nature has awarded me a 5-star TripAdvisor review. My garden is like a wildflower jungle, so it's full of insects, slugs and snails, great tits, song thrushes and hedgehogs. Apart from inviting the local sheep to mow it in winter, I pretty much let Mother Nature run riot. She knows what she's doing.

I also chatted to my former lecturer, Nigel Brown, about gardens. His garden sounds like a Disney animation – it's all beautiful wildflower meadows with swallows swooping and red squirrels bouncing around. He thinks that getting a garden survey is a great place to start because it helps you identify the plants, soil and conditions you've got, which you can use as a basis for wildlife improvement. Nigel's not against mowing a lawn – Nigel has grandchildren, so he appreciates how important that is – but emphasizes, 'As long as a small part of it is not tidy, that's the key.' Thankfully, Nigel reinforced my let's say 'relaxed' approach to gardening, assuring me, 'We're all far too tidy when it comes to gardens, Hamza. Wildlife needs mess!'

Nigel's mowing techniques up at Bangor University's Treborth Botanic Garden did make me chuckle. I remember walking into the garden very early one spring morning and thinking that whoever had cut the garden must have had a few bevvies – there were all sorts of snaky lines and doughnuts here and there! It turns out that one of Nigel's favourite activities was the first mow of the year when he had the chance to create these new shapes in the meadow which were going to be there for the next five or six months. So he'd play around with imaginative shapes and pathways. He found that maximizing the perimeter of each wildflower plot was a smart move, because 'The first 50cm (20in) or so of any meadow plot is the most interesting – the light levels are higher and you can really see the visiting insects,' he told me, adding, 'boundaries are brilliant!' In the wildflower meadows at Treborth, rabbits kept the more thuggish plants in check, which created growing space and light for smaller species, thus increasing plant diversity. The rabbits also nibbled the meadow borders, creating extra diversity as they excreted the seeds of different wildflowers they had munched on elsewhere. I remember the meadow edges had these stunning bee orchids, or 'fantastic but fussy little devils' as Nigel liked to call them because they don't like being overshaded or troubled by 'big stroppy grasses'.

I imagined that one field left all as a hay meadow would be the best for a wildflower meadow, because it's one massive place. But Nigel's found that lots of mini corridors is a good way to go if you believe that variety is the spice of life, as I certainly do! There were about 130 species of plant in the meadows at Treborth, all of which had arrived naturally. As Nigel explained: 'That's far more than the total number of plants and ferns in the mixed woodland. That gives you some idea of the incredible biodiversity of meadows.'

★ ★ ★

When the charity Butterfly Conservation released their report in 2022 about the state of butterflies in the UK, it made me wince, but sadly, it wasn't a surprise. If you ask anyone born in the 1980s or before whether they think there are more butterflies around now or when they were young, there's only going to be one answer. I've seen the change in my lifetime. There's that moment just before an official report comes out when you think it might be a better picture than we had thought, but sadly not in this case. Around 80 per cent of butterfly species in the UK have declined since the end of the 1970s. The species that rely on wildflowers in heathland, moorland and peat bogs are the ones that have been hardest hit, because we've squeezed and squeezed their habitats. Species like the Adonis blue and the swallowtail – two spectacular British butterflies that look like they belong in the Indonesian rainforest, alongside birds of paradise. And then there are the butterfly species that are susceptible to warming temperatures. The Scotch argus is common in the Highlands, but its range used to include northern England. It's now only found in two sites in England. The last Big Butterfly Count (run by Butterfly Conservation and held towards the end of July and beginning of August each year) revealed that several UK butterflies are moving their range northwards. There's usually a sense of excitement when a species expands into a new area, but in this case, they're moving north because of climate change. The trouble is the plants they need to survive on can't follow them.

But you know me by now – I'll find a chink of light in a darkroom! And I'm pleased to say that there are stories of hope fluttering on the breeze. Some are the product of butterflies' own resilience, adaptability and ingenuity;

others are due to smart, kind folks intent on bringing British butterflies back from the brink.

Two iconic and beautiful species that are bucking the downward trend without much help from us are the peacock and the comma. The attribute they both share is that they are 'generalists' rather than specialists that rely on a specific habitat. Peacocks are strong fliers, naturally nomadic and long-lived for butterflies, allowing them to adapt to the flowers and other food sources that are available depending on the season. Their numbers are up 176 per cent in 2023 compared to 2022 according to the Big Butterfly Count. In the last decade or so, they're much more common on my side of the English–Scottish border, including in the Scottish islands. Around the 1850s, the comma was only found along the English–Welsh border, but it bounced back after shifting its taste from hops (which were declining) to nettles, which proved to be a very good shout. If you've never seen a comma before, it's a work of art of a butterfly – the most stunning interpretation of a decaying autumn leaf you can imagine, with its camouflaged orange, brown and black colours and scalloped edges that form two comma-shaped ridges.

The peacock is just a marvel and it's got more tricks up its sleeve than a magician. No one remembers what the underside of a peacock looks like, and that's exactly the point – it just looks like a dead leaf. And then, when the wings come down, you see the Superman outfit underneath Clark Kent's suit. Its two beautiful sets of eyespots look like the tail feathers of a peacock, thought to confuse (or just dazzle) predators. And if the two sets of eyes don't do the trick, when it rubs its wings together, they make a hissing sound, baffling predators further. In addition to hissing, a part of its forewing emits ultrasonic 'clicks', which could be a very specific deterrent against bats. Most creatures have one defence mechanism or two at a push, but the peacock has four. It's built to survive.

Many people come up to Ardnamurchan and Mull to see the white-tailed eagles and golden eagles. Others come specifically for the otters or to photograph a lone stag among the moorland. And there are some who travel far and wide to spot rare butterflies. I'm pleased to say that our unique peninsula is one of only a handful of places where you might find the chequered skipper. Skippers are a family of butterflies that are named for their flying style, which reminds me of someone who's constantly jiggling their leg. They've got larger compound eyes and thicker-set bodies than other butterflies. Also, unlike other butterflies, skippers have these antennae that are hooked at the end, which some folks say look like crochet needles. They remind me of tiny king cobras rearing their head and warning you that they're about to strike.

One of the reasons the chequered skipper is so unusual is that no other skipper has the distinctive chequered pattern of bright-yellow patches on the upper side of its wings. Sadly, its numbers fell rapidly in the 20th century and it was declared extinct in England in 1976, with its last known sites very close to my parents' in Northamptonshire. Until very recently, you could only find it in western Scotland, but thanks to the expertise and ingenuity of the folks at Butterfly Conservation, they've been successfully reintroduced in England. They kept the reintroduction location a secret, which is a tricky task, because typically, everyone involved in a reintroduction project has been working on it for many years and they're too excited to keep it to themselves! But in this case, secrecy is the secret to success because you need to give a species time to become acclimatized to their new habitat, build up resilience and reproduce. And all this hard work has paid off because their numbers are stable enough in this location that lepidopterists (butterfly fans) can safely come and find them. It turns out that the location they chose was the magnificently named Fineshade Wood in Northamptonshire, which was a former chequered skipper stronghold. It's a species that's quite dear to me because there's no other species in the land whose principal strongholds are right outside my front door, and right outside my mum and dad's front door. What are the chances?

I saw my first chequered skipper in long, boggy grass on the edge of a patch of woodland, while I was hiking up to Ben Hiant, the 528-m (1,732-ft) extinct volcano that looms over the west side of the peninsula. It turns out that the range of the chequered skipper had been expanding westwards along the Ardnamurchan peninsula and on to Mull, where they were first seen in 2022. It's a rare success story, especially because their numbers have increased by 87 per cent in the past 20 years.

Other species in this part of the world haven't fared so well, though, like the corncrake. The corncrake is a bird that you might never have heard of. And until a few years ago, it was looking like you might not get the chance to because their numbers were falling so sharply. When I first moved to Ardnamurchan, nearly 15 years ago, you knew summer was on the way when the corncrakes arrived. No bird announces its arrival like the corncrake, let me tell you! They turn up in the middle of the night, sometime in late April, and the males basically start calling about 20,000 times a night. That sounds like I've just thrown in a number for dramatic effect, but that's actually the approximate number of calls. It's no exaggeration to say that this call is one of the most unusual sounds in the entire animal kingdom. Imagine the sound of an especially loud taser with the regularity and oomph of a dance-music beat and you're close to the 'crex, crex' sound they make. And they do it with their beak open and head raised to the sky, a bit like a Pez dispenser.

The corncrake belongs to the rail family, which includes more common birds like coots and moorhens. If you can imagine a moorhen dressed up like a partridge, you're in the right sort of zone, colour- and size-wise. They fly from central and southern Africa all the way to a few sites on the west coast of Scotland and the Western Isles. Male corncrakes need such a distinctive call because otherwise female corncrakes aren't going to have a hope of finding them, given that they spend their time skulking behind tall vegetation in meadows and hayfields. This makes them an unusual member of the rail family, because almost all the others nest in wetlands, hence the corncrake's nickname 'landrail'. The trouble is, because there aren't many fields where tall vegetation hasn't been cut back, their breeding habitat has been seriously squeezed. Plus, corncrakes only live for a couple of years, so it's vital that they find a place to breed and raise their chicks safely before moving on. They used to be widespread across Scotland in summer, but by the mid-2000s, there were only a few hundred left. When numbers of calling males rose to 1,289 in 2014, hope was kindled, but then they dropped again big time. That was what sparked the Corncrake Calling project to help protect their habitats.

A neighbour of mine (it must sound like I have an impossible number of neighbours, but up on the west coast, anyone within about a mile of me is considered a neighbour!) became part of the Corncrake Calling project recently, and she was given a grant to leave the front of her croft alone (i.e. nice and messy) as a corncrake habitat area. In these stretched times, that is a good way to encourage people to join an initiative like that – being compensated for putting aside 20 per cent of the land they use to make their living. There's an area between my house and the lochan (little loch) that I'm hoping to turn into a corncrake habitat next year, so I'm answering the call too!

* * *

There's been a lot of talk about reintroducing apex predators to Scotland to help tackle the overpopulation of deer and the impact their overgrazing has on the landscape. It's hard to imagine now, but wolves were once really common in the UK. But they were considered a serious threat to both livestock and travellers, so from around 1000 CE, their numbers took a nose-dive. January was nicknamed 'wolf month' and hunting season continued until 25 March. In 1281, King Edward I ordered the complete extermination of wolves from England. It didn't work in the way that he intended, but their numbers never recovered. Legend has it that the last wild wolf in the UK was shot by Sir Ewen Cameron of Lochiel near the village of Killiecrankie in the Highlands in 1680. It was the cause of some celebration, largely because wolves had been cast as villains for thousands of years. I'm afraid the Bible and the Qur'an don't do them any favours, and nor do 'Little Red Riding Hood' or 'The Three Little Pigs'!

Wolves are another 'keystone' species, because they are the vital piece that holds a habitat together. We've hunted wolves to extinction in the UK, and that means we've altered the balance of the ecosystem. And we can see the impact of our actions today. Deer numbers are at their highest level for 1,000 years, and while they're undoubtedly beautiful creatures, the damage to the ecosystem that they're causing in the UK is serious. Deer strip the bark off older trees, which kills the trees. They also eat the understorey at the edge of woodland, and that's one of the reasons that birds like nightingales and blackcaps are declining so rapidly. They also eat cereal crops, especially in the east and south-west of England.

Another big benefit of a 'keystone' species is that its presence changes the behaviour of their prey. It creates a 'climate of fear', which I appreciate sounds horrendous (!), but in this instance, it's vital. It means that a wolf's prey is more vigilant than usual, and is far less likely to overgraze because it will continue to move. In Yellowstone National Park, where wolves were famously reintroduced, willow and aspen trees returned to riverbanks. A study by biologists at the University of Wisconsin revealed that the number of collisions between vehicles and deer had fallen by 24 per cent. This is partly because the deer population had reduced but also because wolves navigate using features like roads and pipelines, and that means deer stay away from them.

While the lynx and wolf reintroduction debate continues, we do have a creature that is in some ways performing a similar role. And while they're much misunderstood, they're having a positive impact on the Scottish landscape. And it's the human! My friend Jack Ward is one of them – he's a ranger and ecologist but also a professional deer stalker. 'Stalker' is a confusing term because people tend to think of killing deer for sport. That's not what Jack does. He is essentially an apex predator. His job is to monitor and manage deer in the Cairngorms so they're not permanently damaging the landscape by overgrazing. The deer aren't the villains in this story, though, as Jack explained to me: 'The deer are a vital part of this landscape and we really need them. They can help shape the regenerating woodland through light and sporadic browsing, which encourages young trees to grow in a more ecologically complex way, as they become more twisted and dense, producing more habitat for invertebrates and birds. Everyone talks about beavers as ecosystem engineers but deer are arguably much more so, because unlike beavers, deer roam everywhere.'

While part of Jack's role does involve shooting deer to keep their numbers at a healthy, sustainable level, it's not the only role of a predator. 'My presence in the landscape makes the deer behave naturally, with their eyes up looking for signs of a predator,' he told me. Jack provides that vital climate of fear that makes the deer move through the landscape again rather than hammering areas of regenerating woodland. And when the deer are always on the move, not only do they munch on seeds and then transport them in their droppings, but seeds also attach themselves to the deer's fur, so the deer are constantly moving seeds around the landscape. This is part of the reason that plants and trees start growing. So you can see how Jack's role is hard to define. He's really in the business of habitat restoration.

One of the habitats that Jack spends a lot of time in is also one of the rarest and most unfamiliar in the UK. It's known as montane scrub – the area of shorter vegetation where taller trees have basically reached their altitude limit. So you find low shrubs and dwarf trees (which only reach about 50 per cent of regular size) like willows, dwarf birch and juniper. Jack can see the impact his work is having on this landscape, because suddenly, dwarf trees seem to have miraculously appeared. What's really happening is that these dwarf trees are no longer being munched as soon as they creep above the height of the heather. It's a similar situation with the peatland in the montane scrub – it's now looking so much healthier because large numbers of deer aren't constantly grazing and trampling.

Jack told me about an area of 120 willow trees that Cairngorms Connect – the habitat restoration partnership that Jack works for – replanted and monitored with camera traps. They began to thrive within a year, and by year three, they were growing catkins – long clusters of tiny flowers. That's such good news because that means they'll be reproducing naturally. The willows were getting nibbled by mountain hares, but it turns out that's not such a bad thing. They conducted an experiment by covering some of the willows with wire-mesh cages – and it turned out the uncaged ones grew faster. 'The trees were compensating for that low level of browse and going bananas growth-wise. It's such a cause for celebration,' Jack said. 'This is probably the only place in the UK that predator and prey – herbivore and plant – are living side by side and benefiting each other.'

Cairngorms Connect have been asking staff, volunteers, farmers, herders and the wider local community to help replant the willows, and it's been a lovely success story. Dozens of people turn up. 'It's a properly joyous day,' Jack said. 'By the end of the day, we've planted 4,000 willows. It's really good to just get local people meeting and chatting, and it's all through this effort to try and get a habitat kick-started.'

The plant reintroductions are so exciting and it must feel so rewarding for all the volunteers and locals who contributed. And it brings the promise of something even more exciting – that moment when animals decide that they like the look of the place. A year ago, the Cairngorms National Park reintroduced a pair of beavers! 'It feels like yesterday I was driving a young male and female up in a quad bike, opening the cages and saying, "Up you go, little beavers!"' Jack told me. As I know only too well from down in Longleat, beavers don't hang about, and in July 2024, the female gave birth to a kit. The last time a wild beaver had been born in the Cairngorms, Leonardo da Vinci was still making finishing touches to the Mona Lisa!

Wildcats have returned to the Cairngorms and so much behind the scenes has taken place to bring our

Highland tigers back, not least the strong community support. 'They've done better than we could have possibly imagined,' Jack told me, delighted. Who doesn't love a wildcat? The beavers and wildcats have really caught the media's attention and that's helping to drive up visitor numbers to the Cairngorms. And when that happens, people start to discover the other treasures we have up in Scotland. I can hear my friend Erica McAlister telling me off for focusing too heavily on cute mammals and ignoring insects, so I try to remember the rare dark bordered beauty moth, which seriously lives up to its name, looking like a cross between a stunning autumn leaf and the kind of elegant ladies' fan you might see on *Bridgerton*. The Highland Wildlife Park have been breeding these beautiful creatures and now they're starting to release them. 'I had a lovely evening recently placing caterpillars onto aspen shoots,' Jack told me, truly a man of many talents. 'It's just such an exciting place to be at the minute, for me and for wildlife.'

People like Jack give me hope that humans and nature can thrive together when we work hard. And the great thing about nature is that there's always something new to discover – and there's even more off land.

Chapter 7

Coastlines

———

One of the things I love most about the coastlines of the UK is that it feels like you're on an island within an island. Take Cornwall, for example, with its quirky towns, or the leafy, charming quaintness of south Devon with its sheltered bays and cobblestone cottages. It feels similar to my home in the western Highlands. Both coastlines are dominated by the Atlantic, and that makes you feel small – and I mean that in a good way! – because you can't help but feel humble when you're watching mighty waves break on the rocks. There are so many things that humans have harnessed and learned to control. But here, you truly feel the raw power of Mother Nature. You've got to be a pretty rugged sort to love a rugged landscape. In a harsh winter, you're not going anywhere. But that's what the pub's for, with a roaring fire and a rousing welcome. In the UK, the prevailing wind comes in from the Atlantic. That's why on the west coast, you often see trees bent towards the land.

One thing you see washing up on beaches a lot is a bright-white bony object that's about 15cm (6in) long. When I show one to people, especially kids, some of them will recognize it and tell me it's a cuttlebone. They might also tell me that it smells fishy, which it does (!), or that they're used to feed caged birds. But what always surprises people is when you show them a picture of the creature that it comes from: the cuttlefish. It looks like it belongs on a tropical reef but it's just off the UK coast. And when you describe some of the unique qualities the common cuttlefish possesses, it starts to sound like one of the Avengers.

The common cuttlefish looks like a squid, and like a squid, it has eight arms and two tentacles, big eyes and a mouth with a beak-like jaw which can easily crack open the shells of crabs and molluscs. Like other cephalopods (the family including octopuses and squid), it has three hearts, two of which pump blood to the gills, while the other circulates oxygenated blood (blue-green in colour) to the rest of its body. Here's where they start to get pretty special. Cuttlefish have got millions of cells called chromatophores – tiny sacs filled with pigment that work like pixels in a TV. Each of these cells receives independent instructions from their brain to alter its colour and reflectiveness, and they can do this in literally the blink of an eye. And cuttlefish are the full 3D package because their bodies are covered in bumps and ridges so they can change texture as well, to almost completely match their surroundings.

It is mesmerizing to watch, and 'woah, what the hell is that?!' is exactly what they want both prey and predators (dolphins and sharks, mainly) to be thinking. Males also use the full 3D show to attract a mate. This gets ridiculously sophisticated in a species called the mourning cuttlefish, which can use the side of its body facing the female to perform a dazzling courtship display, while using the other side of its body to mimic a female cuttlefish, so as to confuse a rival male! In order to master this colour- and texture-changing wizardry, they've got some of the most extraordinary brains of all invertebrates. Ironically, cuttlefish (like other cephalopods) only have one type of photoreceptor in their eyes, which means that they're colourblind and can't appreciate their own technicolour show in the way that we can!

The common cuttlefish can weigh up to 4kg (9lb) (that's around the same as a Yorkshire terrier) so they're chunkier than you might imagine, which does make them a particularly tasty morsel for a dolphin or a shark. But they've got to catch these colour-changing, shape-shifting, surprisingly swift creatures, who can also squirt out brown ink to distract and disorient anything pursuing it. This reddish-brown ink is called sepia, and it's been used for hundreds of years for writing and painting, although artificial versions of sepia have mostly replaced the need to harvest their ink sacs. So, when you're adding a sepia filter to a photo on your phone, spare a thought for the originator: the common cuttlefish.

You might be lucky enough to see one in shallow waters in spring where they come to breed. But if you don't, you'll know they're around, because the one thing that remains, after a common cuttlefish has lived its short 1–2-year life, is the white cuttlebone. It's much more than food for a budgie or a tortoise. During its lifetime, the cuttlefish could fill that chambered structure with gas or liquid to control its depth in the water. It's like the ballast tanks that allow a submarine to submerge.

For all these reasons, I'm counting the common cuttlefish as one of our most underrated creatures. The only thing it's got going against it is its name, because it's not a fish and who on earth knows what a cuttle is? Apparently it comes from an old Germanic word meaning 'bag'. I'm already bored! Come on, guys – we can do better than that. We need something that's going to get kids interested, so I'm going for 'shimmering sea chameleon' from now on. No one's going to forget that one!

★ ★ ★

I love walking along the UK's coastlines, and I now seem to be the guy people go to if they want to know anything about white-tailed eagles, who often hunt along the coast. I don't mind as I love telling people about these fantastic birds, but I'm still learning, and white-tails will still act in ways that surprise me. One day, I remember seeing a white-tail carrying a fish with a distinctive zebra colour pattern which told me it was a mackerel. That had me wondering how she'd managed that because mackerel don't tend to come close to the shore, where the white-tails hunt. Maybe it was a case of right place at the right time? But then, one day I saw exactly how she'd managed it.

A group of gannets were doing their incredible plunge-diving trick where they fly towards the water at breakneck speed before folding their wings in at the last millisecond and entering the water like a spear. I saw one catching a mackerel, but that was only half the battle, because there was a white-tail on the gannet's tail. After being harassed by a bird that big and powerful, the gannet coughed up the fish as a sacrifice, because then the white-tail takes it back to its nest and the gannet can try again, this time unmolested. I couldn't believe what I'd just witnessed, though. My beloved elegant white-tails were pirates! Another day I was filming and I was amazed to see what looked like a tropical fish in a white-tail's talons. There were two possible reasons. Either I'd finally spent too long in the hide and had lost my mind, or the white-tails were now nicking fish from aquariums. Then as I got a better view through my binoculars, I recognized the fish as a cuckoo wrasse, probably the UK's most beautiful native fish. I knew she hadn't caught it herself, though, so I wondered who she'd robbed. A few days later, I got my answer when I saw a female otter munching on a cuckoo wrasse. And then, unbelievably, a white-tail swooped in from behind and grabbed the fish in her talons. Daylight robbery!

We get wrasse in Scotland's coastal waters and they're sought after by salmon farms who use them to eat the sea lice off farmed salmon. That way, they don't have to use as many chemical treatments. One of my neighbours – Cookie – was a wrasse fisherman who sold his catch to the farms. But now, to keep up a steady supply of wrasse and to save money in the long term, wrasse are being farmed too. So we've got a situation where fish are being farmed to help keep other farmed fish free of parasites. It's just all so convoluted. Wild salmon are less likely to fall victim to sea lice, but the trouble is, infestations spread from farms into the sea, which affects migrating wild salmon. There's also the ecological graveyard under fish farms caused by uneaten food waste, fish faeces and chemical treatments. That's a toxic combination because it causes nitrogen and phosphorus to collect in large quantities, and that's what leads to algae growing beyond control, contaminating the water and killing animals. If there was an open-net pen salmon farm in the River Thames by Westminster Bridge, it would attract much more attention. But because it's in the remote Highlands, it's a case of out of sight, out of mind.

I think that rather than investing so much money into salmon farming, we should be spending it on protecting wild salmon so they can go back to leaping up the rivers. They've just taken steps along these lines in British Columbia, Canada, banning open-net pen salmon farming so they can protect the wild salmon populations. A victory for the planet over profit.

So poor old wrasse are being hit from three sides – from otters, eagles and humans! Four types of wrasse are common in the seas around the UK, and two of them – the ballan wrasse and the cuckoo wrasse – are used as 'cleaner fish' in salmon farms. These two are so brightly coloured, they wouldn't look out of place in a tropical coral reef. Female cuckoo wrasse are a beautiful pinky-orange above and turquoise below. Males are even more spectacular, with an all-over electric-blue and orange pattern leading to a bright-blue tail. Cuckoo wrasse eat molluscs and crustaceans and their jaws and teeth are strong enough to break through shells. Ballan wrasse are bigger, at up to 60cm (2ft) in length, and they can tear barnacles off rocks, using teeth located in their throat to crush the shells up. Like the cuckoo wrasse, they have striking markings. Many are a kind of spotted blue on an orange background, but their colours can vary a lot. Like many wrasse species, they begin their lives as females. Some of them change sex later in life depending on the number of males in the local population. They become male if there's a need to, basically. And they're not alone. It turns out about 2 per cent of all fish exhibit some form of hermaphroditism. Some change from male to female; others, like the clownfish, transition from female to male. And some species spend their lives switching back and forth.

★ ★ ★

Over half of the world population of northern gannets nests around UK coasts, and close to 200,000 of them breed across just 14 sites in Scotland. About 40 per cent of the entire global population of grey seals live in UK waters. Come to think of it, maybe the royal coat of arms should feature gannets and seals rather than lions and unicorns! Bass Rock in the Firth of Forth has the biggest gannet colony on earth. And these guys are worth a trip. Seeing a gannet hunting is one of nature's marvels, and it's happening just off our shores. You just see these white missiles hurtling towards the sea at 100kph (60mph).

It's only when you watch the footage in slo-mo that you appreciate their spear-like entry into the water. But even with that skilled dive, they're still having to absorb an incredible impact force. And that takes a skull built like a cross between a crash helmet and an airbag.

It's hard to believe now, with grey seal numbers booming in the UK, but at the turn of the 20th century they were being hunted so widely that only a few hundred were clinging on. It was when the Conservation of Seals Act became law in 1970 in the UK that numbers began to properly bounce back. There are now over 120,000 of them in and around our waters. They're basically apex predators because there are only two orcas resident in UK waters.

The first time you see the whiskery head of a grey seal bobbing around only a few yards from the beach is a magical experience. It feels like they're playing a game of hide and seek with you, ducking under the surface and reappearing somewhere else. I always hear 'ta-dah!' in my head when they do it.

Grey seals are the larger of the two species of seal that we have in the UK, the other being the common seal (also called the harbour seal). Grey seals are actually a lot bigger than most people think. Males can reach up to 300kg (650lb), which is about the same as a male and female lion combined! Females top out at about 200kg (450lb) – the same as a fully grown female grizzly bear. They can live up to 40 years and they've become a kind of safari attraction in the UK, especially along the north and east coast of Norfolk. Grey seal pups are curious, which can cause some memorable encounters with humans. They do sometimes make themselves comfortable on the front of a paddleboard along with its user. I can see why! To them, a wonderfully convenient floating island has come past just when they want to put their feet up! In Hemsby, the customers of the Istanbul Delight kebab house must have thought they'd had a few too many drinks on a Friday night in July 2023 when a grey seal pup wandered along the pavement outside. Around 90 per cent of grey seals in the UK breed at coastal colonies in Scotland but they've also colonized rivers in the UK including the Beaulieu in Hampshire. In February 2024, a grey seal pup was spotted on the banks of the river and it's believed to be the first time this has happened in Hampshire waters.

How do you tell grey seals apart from common seals? The fact that a grey seal is a lot bigger won't help you if you see one by itself, so I go by the shape of their faces. Adult grey seals have a long, sloping face with a long, protruding ('roman') nose that juts out much further than their chin. It makes them look a little bit horse-like or like an English bull terrier. If you're quite close to the seal, its nostrils are a really good distinguishing feature. A grey seal has parallel slits for nostrils, whereas a common seal has V-shaped nostrils that are much closer together and sometimes appear to touch. Common seals are also spottier and 'cuter', with more petite faces that remind me of a pug. Grey seals like rocky islands and shores and seem to prefer the northern and western shores of the UK, but you can see them all over our coasts. The best time to see them is between October and January when grey seal cows (females) come ashore to give birth and then spend three weeks weaning their pups. If you see a seal pup with a bright-white fur coat, it's a grey seal, and these guys need to shed this fur before they're able to swim. Common seals are completely different. They give birth in the summer, usually in shallow water, and their pups are happily swimming only a few hours after they're born. They don't have white fur coats – they shed it in the womb, so they're ready to slip into the sea straight away!

Grey seal pups are especially vulnerable in the first three weeks of their lives when they're on the beach. Mama seals get frightened off by humans and dogs and that means the pup won't be getting milk often enough. If she's continually scared away, she might abandon the pup. It's tempting to go and approach a beautiful white seal pup, but it's the worst thing you can do. Touching a seal pup is a big no-no because it means the mum will immediately desert them. And dogs absolutely have to be kept on lead, because if a dog comes into contact with a seal pup, the scent of a dog might also cause the mum to abandon it. Also, although they look adorable, they can bite if you get too close. If you suspect that they're injured, there are some amazing folks out there who specialize in rescuing seals in the UK.

In 2023 I went to film grey seals at Donna Nook, a national nature reserve on the Lincolnshire coast, where large numbers of grey seals come to breed in autumn. They've spent the summer at sea by themselves happily hoovering up fish, eels, crustaceans and molluscs and then suddenly the beach is packed with spotty grey seals. The incredible moment is when that first little white fluffball appears, and then another, and another. The whole team got to watch the pups do everything for the first time. The hungry first feed, that joyful first scratch, the playful rolling over. I felt like an uncle all over again! They pack on the pounds in the first three weeks of their lives, gorging on their mother's milk, which is 50 per cent fat. (Just to put that in perspective, whole cow's milk that you get from the shops is 3.25 per cent fat, and double cream is around 48 per cent fat.) They need all the milk they can get, because after three weeks, the pups are left to their own devices because the mothers go straight back into heat and breed again! So, the birthing season is basically also the mating season, which means that the beach is complete chaos. Well, chaos and harmony combined because you've got three different activities going on simultaneously. First, you've got these cute little pups calling for and being nursed by their mums; then you've got males barking and brawling, rearing up and tearing chunks out of each other's blubbery necks; and finally there are the paired-off couples getting it on. And on top of that, when we were filming all of this, a Chinook helicopter flew just over us (due to the site being used by the Ministry of Defence) and landed further up the beach. All in all, it was a full-on sensory experience like nothing I've ever encountered!

The best part was when the males started doing something known as 'aquaplaning'. Imagine a 300-kg (650-lb) specimen pulling out the worm dance move, performed at serious speed, before he puts his head down and glides along the slippery, muddy surface towards another male, who's checking out one of his females. It was like watching a giant game of curling. They're so fluid and agile in the water, but the same can't be said when they're on land, where they become slithering, blubbery blobs that move awkwardly with this wobbly plopping sound. It's only on land, when they're on a beach in front of you, that you appreciate how big these guys are.

I was paddling a kayak when a huge grey seal bull started bobbing around just a few feet away from me. It doesn't matter how many animals you've been around – seeing a giant water dog suddenly appear in front of you in a completely featureless expanse of water does test your constitution! I told myself that he's not going to cause me any harm – I know he won't, he's a seal – but when you're in the presence of a 300-kg (650-lb) heavyweight, you do start to question your knowledge. When our eyes met, he got a bit scared and dipped below the surface. I started paddling slowly away, but the seal decided that the safest place for him was directly behind me, in my slipstream, which wasn't great for a cameraman desperate to shoot some footage. One of my friends, in another kayak, told me to paddle backwards, which was a really smart move because then the seal moved in front of the kayak and we could get a proper ogle at him. They're such curious creatures. They're also really smart. Seals have started hiding from orcas by jumping onto people's boats because they know they're going to be safer there.

* * *

About a quarter of all cetaceans (whales, dolphins and porpoises) worldwide are found in Scotland. That means we have 24 different species of whale and dolphin in UK waters, which is incredible. Most people don't know that we have killer whales in Scotland, but we'll come on to them in the next chapter. To learn some more about our remarkable cetaceans, I spoke to my friend Siobhán Moran at the Hebridean Whale & Dolphin Trust (HWDT). She's based on the Isle of Mull, literally just across the water from my house, so I used it as an opportunity to ask all the questions I'd been storing up. That's part of the reason I love my job – I get to ask world experts the kind of things that suddenly come to me in the shower!

I wanted to start simple, though, so I asked her what it is about whales and dolphins that we're all so fond of. 'They're big, charismatic, very intelligent, emotional, and it's very easy for us to feel something when we see them,' she said. She told me that she loves the mystery around whales because we only really see glimpses of them at the surface compared to how much of their lives are spent under the waves. It's true – there's so much we don't know about them. I couldn't help but ask her about her favourite encounter. 'Every whale I encounter is my best encounter with a whale!' she told me. I know that feeling very well – it's the same with me and white-tailed eagles. Siobhán has had some magical moments, though, like being in the middle of the sea ice in Antarctica, and having a humpback whale interact with her for an hour. 'That was just spectacular. I was so excited to see it, and it was fascinated by me. And that kind of connection is remarkable.' But there was another encounter, in the summer of 2024, that Siobhán and I were lucky enough to experience together. It started when Siobhán received a notification that a fin whale was swimming up the Sound of Mull.

The first I heard of it was a voice note from Siobhán. I believe it went: 'Hamza, if you're in Ardnamurchan, get out to the coast. There is a bloody fin whale!' When I heard it, I literally turned my van around. A fin whale can grow up to 27m (90ft) long, making it the second-largest animal in the world. If that wasn't exciting enough, the Sound of Mull is absolutely not the place you'd expect to see one. Plus, fin whales move really quickly, so it's a once-in-a-lifetime moment. I called my Scottish father Chris from the car and we were in his RIB half an hour later, with my friends Niki and Martin in another boat. It was all happening. Chris was trying to locate the whale with his fishfinder sonar equipment; I was flying my drone trying to scope it out from the air. When we finally saw it, with its distinctive ridge along its back, it was phenomenal to witness. Even from a few hundred metres away, the scale of a fin whale is something else. And I could see my house in the background!

Siobhán's seen orcas, humpback whales and a fin whale, but her favourite cetacean is the humble harbour porpoise. And I'm so pleased she told me that because while it's our most abundant cetacean, it's absolutely our most overlooked. Part of that's because they're very fast, surprisingly small at a maximum length of only 1.9m (6⅓ft), and tough to spot because they hardly ever breach the surface. They look similar to dolphins, but they're smaller and stockier and their little rounded heads don't have a beak. Also, they've got a kind of triangular bump for a dorsal fin. 'They aren't as showy as dolphins. They don't like to approach boats. They don't perform big acrobatics,' Siobhán told me. 'But they're extraordinary. They have a hunting success rate of up to 97 per cent. No other vertebrate comes close to that.' It turns out that the UK's most successful predators are dragonflies and harbour porpoises. These guys can eat 550 fish an hour. Perhaps that's why they're not performing tricks like bottlenose dolphins. Their super-fast metabolism means they need to hunt and eat like teenagers – almost constantly. 'They're on a mission,' she added.

You can find them all around the shallow coastlines of the UK. You actually don't have to go far out of Glasgow to see a huge population in the River Clyde. You'll probably hear harbour porpoises before you see them because they make this distinctive, loud chuff noise when they come to the surface to breathe, and it's earned them the nickname 'puffing pig'.

When we think of pollutants, we tend to focus on chemicals and plastics, but there's another type of pollution that seriously affects harbour porpoises: noise. They hunt using echolocation in shallow water, so they can be badly disturbed by sources of noise such as boat engines. 'They need a lot of energy so they need to have a reliable food source and feeding pattern,' Siobhán told me. HWDT volunteers have been recording the impact of noise on harbour porpoises for the past two decades and during that time, fish farms (including in the Sound of Mull) have introduced acoustic deterrent devices (ADDs) to scare off seals. They shared their acoustic data set with PhD student Charlotte Findlay, whose research showed the significant shift in harbour porpoise distribution when ADDs were nearby.

Siobhán told me that Charlotte's research, in combination with a massive petition that was run by communities all across Scotland, has meant that, since late 2021, fish farmers have had to obtain strict licences to use ADDs in Scotland. HWDT volunteers haven't recorded the use of any ADDs during their surveys since 2022, which is a massive win for harbour porpoises. And it all started because passionate volunteers donated their time and efforts to bring the plight of the porpoise into the limelight.

It's usually dolphins who get the limelight, and that's partly because they step right into it! I also wanted to know why bottlenose dolphins ride bow waves of boats but I had never managed to find a concrete answer. 'To be honest, we're not 100 per cent sure,' she said. I could hear myself sighing like a porpoise. 'But I see no reason why these intelligent, sociable animals might not do things just for fun!' That's more like it, Siobhán – that's the answer I was hoping to hear. Plus, it's the one that makes sense if, like me, you've ever watched dolphins mess about with pieces of seaweed, draping it over their fins and trying to keep it away from other members of the pod. You can hear them clicking away: 'Ha ha, can't catch me!'

We actually have the largest bottlenose dolphins in the world in Scotland. It seems that they've adapted to cope with the chilly waters by chunking up. They're up to 4m (13ft) long – that's the same as an old Land Rover Defender. They can also weigh up to 400kg (900lb) – that's the same as two silverback gorillas. And you do feel it when you're on a boat. I've had a pod of bottlenose dolphins interacting around us on a RIB (a fast and lightweight boat) in the Sound of Mull, and everyone's bouncing up and down on their seats.

We're extra lucky in the west of Scotland because bottlenose dolphins are found in similar areas to a much rarer and more unusual dolphin, called the Risso's dolphin. They're roughly the same size as our chunky Scottish bottlenoses, but just by looking at their heads, you can tell that they're built for different things. Bottlenose dolphins have a curved head and a stubby beak, whereas Risso's have no beak at all and a big, bulging square forehead. Siobhán told me it's known as a 'bulbous melon', which is a wonderful term because it sounds silly but also conveys exactly what you'd expect. 'It's basically a big ball of fat that is important for echolocation,' she told me, before explaining that the deeper an animal dives, the more bulbous its forehead is. If an animal is in darker waters, it needs a much more accurate echolocation system. Risso's dolphins eat cephalopods like squid and cuttlefish and generally hunt at night, so you can see how they've evolved their distinctive bulbous features. They also don't have any teeth on their upper jaw – they've got between four and fourteen in the lower jaw and use them to grab hold of prey before slurping them down whole.

Another visually distinctive feature of Risso's dolphins is the scarring on their skin. It's partly due to the way they interact, by rubbing their teeth along each other's bodies, but also, the prey that they hunt, like squid, doesn't go down easy! The older Risso's dolphins get – and they can live for over 30 years – the more their scars fade, which is why a really old male might appear to be almost completely white.

Siobhán was quick to praise the hard work of citizen scientists who identified a large population of Risso's dolphins on the north side of the Isle of Lewis. And because of the data they collected, in 2021, the Scottish government designated the area a marine protected area for these special dolphins. 'It's a huge success story for citizen science,' she said. Citizen scientists have also identified bottlenose dolphins mating with Risso's dolphins and creating hybrid babies, with mixed characteristics of both. And that's pretty cool, especially as it's the first time it's ever been known to happen in UK waters.

Chapter 8

Marine

———

A few years ago we were having some incredible marine visitors up in Ardnamurchan, so I decided to set up a WhatsApp group called The Whale-Watching Club. The only trouble was that, as it broadened in members, it broadened in content too. It became less about whale sightings and more of a 'Has anyone seen my cow?' community noticeboard. So we changed the name of that group and I secretly set up another one: The Real Whale-Watching Club. The first rule of The Real Whale-Watching Club is: we only talk about whales and other cetaceans. The second rule of The Real Whale-Watching Club is: we only talk about whales and other cetaceans. An exception came about when we decided that the Northern Lights were also just about okay to talk about.

As I mentioned in the previous chapter, several members of The Real Whale-Watching Club (including me) were lucky enough to see the second-largest whale in the world, the fin whale, in the Sound of Mull. It made me realize that we're pretty spoiled in the UK for marine wildlife, because we also play host to the second-largest fish in the ocean, the basking shark. They can grow up to 12m (40ft) long and 5t in weight. Basking sharks have teeth, but they're absolutely tiny and not used to catch prey. Instead, they swim with their vast mouths open, to filter out plankton from sea water. The sight of a basking shark with its mouth open is extraordinary. Every once in a while they close their mouths, and I'm left wondering how many millions of gallons of sea water have just passed through that shark's gills!

The basking shark gets its name because it spends time feeding slowly at the water's surface. The Western Isles see some of the largest groupings of these guys in summer because that's where the plankton is at. Not so long ago, people were shooting harpoons at them for their blubber and oily liver, which weighs up to a tonne. Now, they're shooting them in a different sense, with drone cameras, to try and unlock some of the secrets of this mysterious, gentle giant. Satellite tracking from 2008 revealed that one basking shark had travelled from the Isle of Man to an area of ocean between Greenland and Newfoundland – a distance of nearly 10,000km (6,000 miles). It also showed us that they travel a lot deeper than we had thought, at up to 1,264m (4,146ft).

One of the best places to catch sight of a basking shark in the UK is between April and October off the western tip of Cornwall. They seem to travel from there along the coast of Wales and up towards the Isle of Man, where they're thought to breed, before heading north towards the Hebrides. In the Inner Hebrides, you'll find Fingal's Cave, a unique nature reserve on the uninhabited island of Staffa. Formed entirely from hexagonal interlinking basalt columns, it is one of the most remarkable sights in the world. And if you're thinking that sounds like the Giant's Causeway on the north coast of Northern Ireland, you're right, because they were both formed from lava flowing out of a volcano roughly 60 million years ago. That's the scientific answer, anyway. There's a more poetic tale that tells of the Irish giant

Fionn mac Cumhaill (Finn McCool), who had some beef with Scottish giant Benandonner after the latter decided that Ireland was his. Finn wasn't happy about it and started lobbing great boulders into the sea. Watching them hit the water, he had a thought, *Why don't I use these boulders to build a causeway between Ireland and Scotland – then I could challenge this guy on his own turf.* Only, Finn hadn't realized how much bigger Benandonner was than him, until he caught sight of him. So Finn came up with a ruse. He left the causeway for Benandonner to find, who took the bait, travelling across to Ireland. Meanwhile, Finn disguised himself as a baby giant, and got his wife to pretend to nurse him. Benandonner was terrified at the thought of how big Finn must have been if his baby was already this huge so he ran away, back along the causeway, and tore it down, leaving only the Giant's Causeway at one end and the sea cave on the island of Staffa at the other.

I've been to Fingal's Cave on my Scottish father Chris's boat, and it's a stunning place. The cathedral-like acoustics inside are legendary and have inspired artists, writers and composers to produce works about it. Staffa is a wildlife haven, famous for its puffins that arrive in early April, find a mate and raise a single chick together before they all leave at the end of July. Black guillemots, northern fulmar and the great skua, which specializes in stealing food from other sea birds, all nest on the island too. Dolphins, porpoises, seals, minke whales and pilot whales can be found in the surrounding waters. As can the basking shark.

The year 2024 was a bumper year for basking shark sightings. The Irish Whale and Dolphin Group (who count basking sharks as 'honorary whales') recorded more whales than they had in their last record year, 2009, and excitingly, this time, more sharks were spotted together. Sadly, it was also a record year for the number of basking sharks washing up on Irish shores, many of which had been entangled in fishing nets and lobster pot ropes.

In 2024, I went on an incredible boat trip with my good friends Niki and Martin – who live just up the road from me – around the small isles of the western coast. Niki is a marine biologist and a science advisor to the UK government specializing in marine mammals in UK waters, so just about the best tour guide it's possible to have the pleasure of travelling with. I've seen so many interactions with cetaceans in and around Ardnamurchan when I'm with Niki and Martin because we pootle along in the RIB. We move fast until we get wind of a sighting, and then we slow right down. They often come to you when you keep a slow, steady pace and direction. You also get a much better view. I remember one time we were travelling at about seven or eight knots and we literally had a conveyor belt of dolphins in our bow. Finally, we realized we needed to be getting home, so we cut the engine but then they just bobbed around and stayed with us for ages! We could all hear them squeaking under the water! It was such a special encounter.

Niki, Martin and I visited Canna, Eigg, Rum, Muck and Soay, the smallest of the small isles. In Soay, we visited the site of a former basking shark fishery that was set up by a man called Gavin Maxwell. Maxwell was a mysterious figure who reads like something from a James Bond book. He was the son of a Scottish aristocrat and grew up with a thirst for adventure. His skills with firearms – he could shoot table tennis balls out of the air – meant he was recruited by British special forces during the Second World War. He trained resistance fighters in occupied France and reached the rank of major but was discharged in 1944.

Just after the war ended, Maxwell bought the island of Soay. There, he started hunting basking sharks, to harvest the very valuable livers. Each liver could produce up to 400 gallons of a yellow-orange oil, which was used to make cosmetics, perfume and artificial silk. Over four years, he and a business partner hunted over 4,000 basking sharks. The business venture didn't work out, and neither did the ownership of Soay, but his experience became the subject of his first book, *Harpoon at a Venture* (1952). Maxwell had always wanted an otter as a pet, and got to realize this dream in 1956, when he was travelling through the salt marshes of Iraq with his explorer and writer friend Wilfred Thesiger. Thesiger managed to find Maxwell a baby smooth-coated otter, who he named Mijbil. Mijbil became the subject of his book *Ring of Bright Water*, which he wrote at his cottage in Sandaig, facing the Isle of Skye. The book sold over a million copies, making Maxwell famous and inspiring a new generation of young naturalists. One of them was already working with Maxwell as an apprentice at his house in Scotland. And his name was Terry Nutkins, who I remember from *The Really Wild Show* in the late 1990s. If you ever wondered why Terry Nutkins had two fingers shorter than the others: one of Maxwell's otters had bitten him.

The basking shark fishery just looks like a ruined old house by the water, but when you see the ramps and remnants of boiler rooms inside, you realize it served a more sinister purpose. It reminded me of the old, rusted metal buildings I visited in Grytviken, South Georgia, which had similar features, used for hooking and dragging the whales and then boiling their blubber. I wondered quite how many sharks must have been in the waters around Soay. I spoke to a fisherman in Dervaig, a little village on the west coast of Mull, and he told me the old saying that there used to be so many basking sharks here that you could walk from the Isle of Mull to the Isle of Tiree without getting your feet wet. At first, this just sounds like a funny old tale – the kind of thing you hear up in the Highlands. But it got me thinking. Basking sharks grow up to around 8m (26ft) long. If Gavin Maxwell caught 4,000 of them, and you laid them out end to end, that works out as 32,000m, or 32km (20 miles). I measured the distance between the western edge of Mull and the eastern edge of Tiree on Google Earth. It's 23.48km (just over 14½ miles). It's not an old wives' tale. You wouldn't get your feet wet!

I've never actually seen a basking shark in the wild, not for want of trying! I went out with Shane from Basking

Shark Scotland, who takes people out to Gunna Sound between the islands of Coll and Tiree. As the oncoming tide hits the two islands, it's thought to funnel the plankton between them, which might explain why it's become such a basking shark hotspot. The cairns of Coll, the rocky outcrop on the north side of Coll, is another place, but even though lots of other folks have seen them, I've never been that lucky. Niki's been in close contact with basking sharks as part of surveys and tagging projects in the Isle of Man and told me, 'They look so prehistoric and when you see them up close – their skin is this beautiful grey mottled colour.'

In December 2020, the Sea of the Hebrides became the first Marine Protected Area (MPA) to give specific protection to basking sharks. And we've been able to learn more about their mysterious movements thanks to the satellite-tags researchers have fitted to basking sharks. 'They're swimming at much deeper depths than they used to be, possibly because that's where the plankton is concentrating,' Niki told me. It could also have something to do with climate change altering the sea temperature, which plankton are very susceptible to. It seems that basking sharks' food of choice, the northern species of copepod (very small crustaceans), are moving further north, so that could be influencing things too. Satellite tagging has been a game-changer. 'Until recently, embarrassingly recently actually, we thought basking sharks sank to the bottom of the sea and hibernated there!' Satellite tagging has revealed that they migrate and form several groups. Some stay around the UK, then maybe head up towards the Faroe Islands; another group seems to go down to the Bay of Biscay; a third migrates to North Africa; and a fourth group makes a bee-line across the Atlantic. One basking shark, as reported in a paper of 2008, travelled 9,589km (5,958 miles) in 82 days, all the way from the Isle of Man to Newfoundland. It's such an exciting time to study basking sharks because we're just starting to unlock some of their mysteries.

* * *

We have a resident pod of orcas in the UK, and that's a wonderful sentence to be able to write. They weren't officially studied until the early 1990s, when ten members of the pod were recorded, who became known as the West Coast Community. Before then, we relied on occasional sightings by citizen scientists off the west coast of Scotland. Fortunately, one orca looked so unique, with the deep triangular indentation near the base of his dorsal fin and the shark-mouth-shaped chunk taken out of his tail, that he became easy to spot. He became much loved and was named John Coe.

In the past few years, only two members of the pod have been seen – John Coe and his pal Aquarius. John Coe is thought to be just over 60 years old, which makes him one of the oldest orcas living in the wild today. Seeing him is a special privilege, and we're very lucky up here in Ardnamurchan, because he pops by our shores more than most. I'm writing this after hearing that he's just been spotted and you should see the excitement levels on the west coast. It's incredible to be part of.

It's ironic that hearing an orca breathe takes your own breath away but that's exactly what happens. It's overwhelming being in the orbit of such a magnificent creature, the scale and majesty of which you just can't convey until you *know*. But it goes beyond *watching* a whale. You feel like they're studying you with the same intensity that you're gazing at them. It's a feeling that only surfaces when you're engaging with highly intelligent mammals, like gorillas, chimpanzees and dolphins. And then there's the fact that John Coe is one of the oldest orcas in the world, born before we landed on the moon. It's a unique privilege to interact with him.

Being on a boat with my friend Niki Clear is a real privilege, especially when the boat contains children or marine muggles. And that's because if Niki spots a dolphin, seal or whale, she'll instinctively want to share the experience with those around her. 'Would anyone like to borrow my binoculars?!' she'll ask. She does it because she knows that that moment could inspire a child forever the same way it did for her. Niki gets involved – and that's exactly what happened one perfectly normal day in Ardnamurchan. It started with dozens of notifications from The Real Whale-Watching Club: John Coe and Aquarius had been sighted off the coast of Oban.

What followed was an incredible relay of sightings as they travelled along the coast and a frantic flurry of activity as everyone tried to get into position to photograph them as they travelled up the Sound of Mull. I wasn't on the peninsula, guttingly, but I was living vicariously through the WhatsApp group. And my adrenaline was pumping like crazy!

Niki and Martin went over to our friend Liz's house, which has the ideal view over the water. Finally their patience was rewarded, as Niki described with bubbling excitement reliving the tale: 'That feeling you get when you see the little cloud of water droplets shooting out from the water's surface is indescribable. You're overflowing with excitement because you know it's about to happen. And then you see the black and the white.' But then a thought struck Niki and she stared at Martin. They both had sea kayaks – why weren't they in the water?!

'So we ran home, squealing, got our kit on, raced to the jetty and high-tailed it out across the sound,' she said. But by the time Niki and Martin had made it out there, they were worried it was too late, until one of the boats following the orcas waved at them shouting, 'The orcas are coming through. The orcas are coming through!!!' And then, about 200m (650ft) away from them, Aquarius surfaced. 'We could hear him breathing,' Niki told me. They watched the huge dorsal fin go up and down a few times and managed to capture it on video. 'Then, directly in front of us was John Coe's distinctive wavy dorsal fin with the triangular notch and the iconic tail fluke. It was absolutely spellbinding.' For many years, the closest Niki got to John Coe was the beautiful line tattoo of him on her left forearm with the distinctive notch on his dorsal fin.

Since she's moved to Ardnamurchan, though, she's now seen him several times, once even from her living room!

I remember the first time I saw John Coe and Aquarius. I was actually on a date with a girl who'd come up to Ardnamurchan to see me. We went out on my motorbike, took the ferry over to Mull and rode over to Glengorm Castle, a few miles to the west of the capital Tobermory, overlooking the Sound of Mull. My phone rang – it was my friend Titch, one of the local fishermen.

'Are you about, Hamza?'

'Ah – I'm not in the village at the moment, Titch. I'm on a date!' I whispered.

'Oooooooh! A date eh?! Well, I'm sorry to tell you that you've missed them again.'

'Missed who, no – the orcas?!'

'Aye – they're coming up the Sound of Mull!'

I could feel my heart pounding away because at that moment, I was on Mull, looking over the sound.

'Where are they, Titch?'

'Just coming past Ardmore Lighthouse.'

'You're joking.'

Ardmore Lighthouse was behind me. I scanned the water and my eyes were immediately drawn to two clouds of water just above the surface, one after the other. It was John Coe and Aquarius. This is why you always carry your binoculars! Next thing I know, Niki's calling me.

'Hamza – where's my scope?'

Niki had kindly let me borrow her scope a couple of days before.

'I'm so sorry! It's in the back of the van and it's locked!'

I'm surprised we're still friends after that.

That was the first and only time I saw John Coe and Aquarius. If the lady I'd been seeing had been a nature fan, that would have been the greatest first date of all time. Unfortunately, though, she wasn't, so it wasn't!

People come from all over the world to try and catch a glimpse of John Coe and Aquarius. I can't tell you how many conversations about them I've had with campervan drivers outside my front gate! So why is it such a bittersweet tale? Well, there are distinct types of orca known as ecotypes, which are almost like different species. They differ in terms of size, appearance, diet, how they forage and how they communicate. Different ecotypes don't interbreed and they rarely interact. The West Coast Community pod is an isolated group of North Atlantic Type 2 orcas. They're roughly a metre larger than others and there's never been any evidence of interaction with any other pods, which would explain why they've become quite inbred. For as long as they've been recorded, there's never been any evidence of a calf.

In 2008, when one of the bulls – Moon – sadly washed ashore on the Isle of Lewis, we were able to discover more about this special pod. Moon's teeth were well-worn, and a minke whale baleen (the bristles in the mouths of toothless whales, used to sieve plankton from water) was found in his stomach, so we were able to confirm that this pod hunts marine mammals. When Lulu, a female member of the pod, tragically died after becoming entangled in creel rope in 2016, the postmortem revealed that the chemical pollution in her body was 100 times the safe threshold. It's well known that high polychlorinated biphenyl (PCB) levels are linked to infertility. It seemed that we had our answer as to why there's never been a calf.

There is some cause for hope, though. The Shetland Islands have become an orca hotspot. We have three groups of semi-resident orcas there and other Iceland-based pods who have been visiting the Shetland Isles in summer and hunting seals. There have also been confirmed sightings of a mystery group of orcas off Skye and even in the River

Clyde. As Niki told me: 'It seems to coincide with John Coe and Aquarius being some distance away – like off the coast of Ireland – so they aren't patrolling their waters.' So while it'll be such a dark day when John Coe and Aquarius leave us, it's possible that another orca pod will take up residence in Hebridean waters. But for now, I'll keep longing for that moment when we get that ping on The Real Whale-Watching Club with the message: 'John Coe and Aquarius are heading home!'

Chapter 9

Highlands

———

When I first came to this part of the world, during a university holiday with my friend Sarah and her family, we drove across the vast boggy wilderness of Rannoch Moor. Then the landscape began to change colour, from the browns and oranges of the moorland to the lush green valleys of Glencoe. Three mountains came into view, which I discovered were known affectionately as the Three Sisters. I was amazed that you didn't even need to hike for several hours to discover a view like this. You could see it from your car! It was at this point that Sarah's dad put on his storybook narrator voice: 'Tell me, Hamza, have you heard of the Glencoe Giant?' I shook my head. 'Legend has it there's a hidden valley behind the three peaks. That's where he lives. And you'll know if he's in or not, because if he is, you'll see the wisp of smoke from his kettle.' I felt like a five-year-old and was loving every minute of it.

After 30 seconds or so of growing anticipation, we rounded a bend and a little more of the landscape came into view. I saw the smoke. 'He's home!' I shouted, like I'd just seen Santa come down the chimney. Now, I knew this was Sarah's dad's party trick, but it didn't matter. You know the story isn't true but when you're experiencing something truly magical, you put that to one side. You want to believe the fairytale. The lingering effect is that whenever I drive through Glencoe, I'm looking to see if the giant's home. I relive that excitement every time, and if I'm with my nieces or godchildren, they'll hear the tale as well. But that's how I live my life. I start each day ready to be filled with wonder. And that'll happen even if I'm in the big city for the whole day. Because at some point I'll look out the window and see something I've never seen before.

On that trip to the west coast of Scotland for the first time, I saw a stag on the top of a small hill just a couple of hundred metres away and you couldn't have curated a more beautiful scene. 'Please stop the car, guys!'

I bellowed. Sarah's family, bless them, got used to me wanting to stop practically every 50 yards to take a picture of every animal I saw.

I remember that once we'd crossed Loch Linhe on the Corran Ferry, I looked at the satnav and saw that we had 44 miles to go. But it said the journey time would be two and a half hours, and there wasn't any traffic showing up on the route. 'I think your satnav's broken, guys!' I said. 'Trust me, Hamza – you'll understand,' Sarah's dad reassured me.

It's 20 years later, and now I'm the one telling my friend Nathan, who hasn't come to see me before up in the west of Scotland, that the satnav isn't broken. It's late summer, and after a lovely but long stretch of filming and presenting, I'm finally homeward bound. I love it when friends come to stay for the first time. Especially those who are nature lovers, because there's a good chance they're going to see a stag, an otter and an eagle – three of Ardnamurchan's big four – on the way home. I can't magic up the biggest of the big four, John Coe and Aquarius.

As we head off the ferry and up the slip road, there are two cars, two caravans and a pick-up truck ahead of me. Like me, they were in the middle lane of the car ferry, and that's the lane you want to be in, because that's the one they always let off the boat first. I can't quite explain it but I have this uncontrollable urge to get home first, and at the moment, we're sixth on the grid. But because I don't recognize any of the four vehicles ahead of me, it means they're all visiting. I'm the only local, and I know this road so well that I can visualize exactly when we'll be able to pass each of them safely. After that, we're home free! I know we're very unlikely to encounter any cars going the same way as me because the ferry only lands on the Ardnamurchan shore every 30 minutes or so. So we've got a clear run home, unless of course someone I know is at a passing place along the way. Then we'll be stopping and chatting until another car appears behind us. And if that car belongs to a local, sometimes they'll get out and join in the chat. It's a community like no other.

We all have our parts to play in each other's lives. It's one of the reasons that Scotland felt like home to me so quickly. And it helped that, in some ways, I had the necessary equipment, because, like a true Scot, I could roll my 'r's. And that's because you roll your 'r's in the Arabic language, and you get pretty good at it when you've got an older brother whose first name is 50 per cent 'r's.

It might sound like a silly thing but it's another little sense of connection between Sudan and Scotland.

We've only been driving for a few minutes, and already we're going past the River Gour along which there's a remnant of the ancient Caledonian Forest. And where you've got ancient pine forest, you'll usually find one of my favourite animals: pine martens. These guys do love a pine tree, but they'll also set up camp in other native woodlands, scrub and rocky hillsides. And they've been known to get into some unexpected places . . .

'Hamza! There's a pine marten living in my attic!' my friend Liz shouts down the phone.

Believe it or not, these are the kind of phone calls I receive up in Ardnamurchan. 'I'll be right over, Liz!' I tell her, and I jump in the van.

We're a close community and I've become a sort of Highlands Dr Doolittle, a title I bear with pride. For those of you who might not know what a pine marten looks like, it looks similar to a stoat or a weasel (like them, it's a member of the mustelid family, which includes otters and badgers), only it's a lot bigger – about the size of a domestic cat. It also, unlike other mustelids, has semi-retractable claws, which makes it a fantastic climber. It's lightning-fast and mainly hunts small mammals and birds.

Our local pine marten started her association with the Ardnamurchan community in Liz's attic, before moving down the road to my attic, but unfortunately she didn't stay there long. She preferred the look of Jeff and Sandra's place, which I tried not to be offended about! One day, I was over at Jeff and Sandra's house for a cup of tea, and not long after, we heard all sorts of scrabbling going on upstairs. Excitingly, there were multiple scrabbles – one properly loud scrabbling and some little scratchings. I smiled because that told me there was a mama pine marten just above us nursing her cubs. In fairness, she couldn't have chosen a nicer house! Rising up through the attic was a lovely warm wood-burning stove flue and lots of insulation to keep it nice and toasty up there. We fed the mum peanuts, which she absolutely loved, so of course she ended up with the name Peanut.

From downstairs, I was able to get an idea of her movements around the attic. There seemed to be one place which Peanut visited at pretty much the same time each day, which I later found out was for good reason – that was the place she'd chosen to do her business.

We'll all creatures of habit! That's how they mark their territory – by pooing in the middle of it. When Peanut headed out on her evening wander, I shimmied up there to set up cameras. When we opened the attic hatch, three ridiculously fluffy baby pine martens peeked their heads over the edge. I gave them a peanut each, which they were delighted about before deciding that they preferred the look of the peanut I'd given to their brother or sister. I'd accidentally started a squabble.

Later that day, I checked out the Vincent Wildlife Trust's advice on constructing a nest box den for the little family out of plywood. Me and my neighbour Tom Bryson knocked it together in no time at all. Peanut took to our creation at first, before deciding that she preferred the more luxurious surrounds of Jeff and Sandra's heated attic. In fairness, if I'd been staying in the presidential suite of a hotel and suddenly the hotel manager was trying to encourage me to accept a single room, I know what I'd be saying!

More and more pine martens are making their dens in people's attics, and you can understand why. I deliberately made my attic a pine marten haven by not fixing one of the roof flashings so they could access it from the outside. For me, seeing as we are the ones who moved into the pine marten's natural habitat, I feel like we owe it to them to share our homes. It's a privilege to provide a home for such a beautiful creature. They're shy but very smart and quick. I remember Peanut discovering that there were chicks nearby in a nest up a tree but deciding not to attack. She waited until they were much plumper so they'd be a more substantial meal for her cubs. That's impressive intellect. Pine martens can change an ecosystem, which makes their reintroduction to Wales in 2015 especially wonderful news. Pine martens hunt squirrels, and especially grey squirrels, who don't seem to be as good at evading them as red squirrels are. And that means that our rare red squirrels are beginning to recolonize areas that grey squirrels had overrun. Between 2019 and 2021, pine martens were reintroduced to England. The Forest of Dean in Gloucestershire was the location, where pine martens had last been seen in 1860. Since then, the pine martens have bred successfully every year and their range is expanding. The hope is that the English and Welsh populations will eventually merge. What a day that'll be!

As I continue my journey from Fort William to Ardnamurchan, I venture beyond the Caledonian Forest remnants. Another 15 minutes to the west and the luxury of a 2-lane A-road is in the rearview mirror. As the road narrows, you can't help but notice how green everything is around you. There are ancient sessile oaks everywhere, along with beeches, birches, willows and hazels. You notice moss and lichen all around. It's a landscape that feels like it loves being alive. It's Atlantic rainforest. I took the Reverend Richard Coles there in 2021 and it was the first time he'd seen a landscape like it. He was completely overcome by its beauty.

As Richard and a lot of my friends discover, it's not uncommon for me to pull over in my van quite suddenly. It means I've spotted an animal, although I'm so excited that I often don't actually communicate that to my friend, so they're sat there wondering what the hell is going on. On one occasion, I saw an otter in Loch Sunart, on the approach to the beautiful village of Salen. So I jumped out and frantically gestured to Nathan to do the same. Then I started barking short sentences at him. 'OTTER! . . . Keep low to the ground! . . . Okay, STOP! . . . Don't move! . . . Okay, it's under – quick, quick, quick!'

Otters pop up at the surface to breathe, before diving back down into the loch. When I see that paddle-shaped tail dip below the water, we're on. You've about

30 seconds to get yourself into position before they come up for air again – hence the excitable rush. Nathan told me afterwards that it was a bit like playing 'What's the Time, Mr Wolf', and I see his point! You run towards them when they're not looking and once they appear again, you freeze. The trouble is the 30-second rule only works if the otter hasn't caught something. If they catch a fish, they'll be up way quicker than 30 seconds. Then they'll pop up on the rocks or on a jetty, take a nibble, have a poo, and then they're back in the water. On this occasion, the otter hadn't caught anything, so we made it on to the edge of a metal jetty. Still crouching, obviously. I could see the otter's spraint (droppings) there, which is easy to miss if you don't know what you're looking for. It's a small, crumbly mass of fish scales, bones and crab shell fragments, and they usually deposit it on a prominent rock near the water's edge. Oddly, it doesn't smell bad. It's actually kind of sweet-smelling, fishy and floral, if you can imagine that!

You can deduce something about the otter by the contents of its spraint. If there are a lot of fish scales in there, you know it's a healthy, active otter because fish are trickier to catch. If the spraint has lots of crab pieces in it, it could tell you that the otter is a little younger or older, or not that healthy, because crabs are much easier to catch. It doesn't always work though because sometimes crabs will be all that's on offer, but it's a helpful pointer. One clue that otters love a particular spot is that amid the grass near the water's edge, you'll find a patch that's a different shade of green from the surrounding grass. It will be a more vibrant shade, because the otter's been pooing on it and otter spraint is as good as any fertilizer.

As we eventually left the otter to it and walked back along the jetty, I saw a lion's mane jellyfish just below the surface near the back of a boat. It's such a beautiful creature. They have these reddish-brown saucer-shaped bells and incredible hair-like flowing tentacles – hence its name. The oldest tentacles are the deepest red in colour. The bell's usually up to 50cm (20in) across and the tentacles up to 3m (10ft) long, but they can grow absolutely massive. The largest one ever recorded had a 2.1-m (7-ft) bell and stretched 36m (120ft) from top to bottom. This remarkable animal isn't actually that uncommon in UK waters between May and October. We only get a few species of jellyfish, but they all look pretty amazing. The moon jellyfish is the most common, with four distinctive circles that you can see through its translucent bell.

After we reluctantly leave this stunning scene and jump back into the van, the single-track road hugs the coastline for the next 19km (12 miles). The scenery changes from Atlantic rainforest, with all of its lush green beauty, to the more varied colours of the open moorland. There are pockets of purple heather contrasting with the rusty orange of ferns that are just starting to go over. Near a passing place, I suddenly see a pair of antlers amid the ferns, so I stop to take a picture. I can't help it. Then the stag bounds away because a van is approaching – it's Ulrich, whose flat-bed van carries the propane gas that people across the peninsula need for their heaters.

Another 15 minutes along the shoreline of Loch Sunart, we pass the turreted pillars and old stone gatehouse of Glenborrodale Castle on the right. On the left, we get our first glimpse of the Isle of Mull. Soon we pass the Ardnamurchan whisky distillery and I think of my neighbour Ricky, who works as one of the tour guides there. He's a kind, poetic soul and a man of many talents. With 22 years of experience in the army, he's also our village's first responder. If there's an emergency, Ricky's the man you want there. If ever we need someone to stand up and say a few words, like to address the haggis on

Burns Night or to bring the community together at a time of grief, Ricky is the person who steps up. He's also very passionate about archaeology, and has been involved in uncovering Bronze Age and Viking burial sites in the west of Scotland. In fact, Ricky became the first person in a thousand years to suffer an injury at the hands of an ancient Viking when he cut himself on a sword that he'd discovered! Like me, Ricky loves the wildlife up in this part of the world.

When I get home, I'll visit Ricky to check on the injured male raven he'd rescued a couple of weeks ago. Ricky's named him Dubhaidh (pronounced 'Doo-ey') and has built him a special enclosure in his garden to help him recuperate. When Ricky told me he'd rescued a raven, I knew exactly where he'd come from because I can see his nest on Ben Hiant, the highest peak on the peninsula, from my front window. It started off as a buzzard nest, not a huge one, and then the pair of ravens added to it. They lined it with sheep fur and orange baling twine that you could see a mile away. By the end of January, they start building their nest back up again after the winter and they have eggs in early February. To people who love wildlife, they're very much part of our community.

We round a corner and I immediately notice that Titch the fisherman has moved his boat into one of the sheltered bays. It sounds like a small thing, but that moment marks the end of summer because the weather's already started to turn. We pass the llamas in a field owned by Les, so of course his name has become 'Llama Les'. When you're in a small community and two or more people share a first name, they're always going to end up with a nickname. And that nickname often involves what they do day to day. There's more than one Pete, so one of them has become 'Soily Pete', because he moves a lot of earth around with his diggers. Likewise, there are three Alastairs, so somehow they've become Titch, Pinky and the General.

We drive past local landmark, St Columba's Well, named after the Irish missionary who spread Christianity to Scotland. Legend goes that in the sixth century, Columba landed at nearby Camas nan Geall (Bay of the Strangers) and came across a sick baby. So he blessed a rock, which then bubbled up with pure water, which he used to baptize him. The well is still running, and it tastes great.

The road continues upwards, giving us a spectacular view of Camas nan Geall. From this beautiful bay, the road heads north and into the hills, where the golden eagles nest. I've spent days and days sitting and watching golden eagles here, because there's a ridgeline that the prevailing westerly winds blow against, forcing the air upwards and giving the eagles a free ride. The goldies come in low over the bay and then rise up directly above you. It's a stunning place to witness such a stunning bird.

Over on the left, rising out of the north-western tip of Camas nan Geall, is a river whose meanders are so beautifully formed, they look like something out of geography textbook. After that, you can follow the river by the ancient trees that line the increasingly steep-sided banks. The difficult terrain means that the trees that have taken root there are protected from deer and sheep. And when you look the other way, you can see the impact the deer have had on the rest of the land. It's a vast basin of moorland, with probably 1,500 deer. And while it is a picturesque landscape, and a stag in the craggy uplands is a staple image of the Highlands, what I see is overgrazing. This isn't what the Highlands would have looked like. And I know this because close to where I live is an area of moorland that has been fenced off for the last 20 years to prevent deer and sheep grazing. Here you'll see shrubland and young broadleaf woodland. It's all green.

We rumble across the cattle grid and we're out of the protected area. Then, all you can see on your left is a dense plantation of Sitka spruce. Sitka spruce plantations are a spiky topic. The tree is native to the west coast of North America and was introduced to Great Britain in 1831. In the 1970s and 1980s, Sitka was grown all over the Highlands, including over peatlands, which caused an outcry from conservationists because it was outmuscling native species. It was only later on that we realized how important peatlands were for sequestering (storing) carbon – which they do far more efficiently than trees in fact.

Looking at this monoculture of a commercial Sitka spruce plantation makes me sad as I'm someone who has always believed that variety is the spice of life. And yet Sitka spruce now accounts for 43 per cent of all Scottish woodlands.

To me, it feels like the advocates of Sitka spruce plantations tend to either have a financial interest or prioritize potential economic benefits over ecological ones. I'm not against Sitka spruce as a tree – in its native habitat in North America, it can live for 700 years and provides food, shelter and nesting sites for all sorts of creatures, including bald eagles. Plus, Sitka's carbon-storing ability is a cause for celebration. It just needs to be planted with care, attention and diligence. And most importantly, not in a monoculture. Even if you don't give a monkey's about the environment and are just looking at it from a financial perspective, a monoculture is vulnerable to being wiped out by a disease or pest. For me, you just need to spend some time in an area of Atlantic rainforest, and then do the same in a Sitka spruce plantation. You'll notice a big difference. There's life all around you in Atlantic rainforest. There's sound. Whereas Sitka spruce plantations feel like cemeteries – they're silent, symmetrical and sad places. And that's because their dense planting means that light doesn't reach the forest floor, so there's very little growing there. Our native Atlantic rainforest is a complex community of plants, animals and fungi that have been coexisting for thousands of years. Non-native conifers just don't provide the resources our native wildlife needs. And you just need a pair of eyes and ears to witness that. Thankfully, there has been some progress in the right direction. On 1 October 2024, a new UK Forestry Standard came into effect. The maximum proportion of a single species of tree in a new woodland has been reduced from 75 per cent to 65 per cent, which will hopefully diversify the range of species.

As we pass the plantation, the road leads down towards Kilchoan. The turning for the ferry terminal, which takes you across to Tobermory, on the Isle of Mull, is just ahead. When I came up to Kilchoan for the second time, only two weeks after I'd first come here with my friend Sarah and her family, I lived in the back of my car by the ferry terminal, so it holds a lot of memories for me. I tried to make it look as though I wasn't living in my car, so I'd be sure to drive off before the first ferry of the morning arrived. What I didn't know until many years later was that everyone in the village knew I was living in my car. I figured that the locals would probably be wondering why this black dude with a big camera was always there, and, sure enough, people started taking an interest. One of the early encounters I remember went like this:

'What are you up here photographing?'

'I'm here to find the wildcats, deer, otters and everything!' I said, with the excitable enthusiasm and naivety of a 20-something who was on an adventure into the unknown.

'You might like to know that there's a white-tailed eagle nest, just . . . there,' the guy said, pointing at a rocky face in the distance.

'What?!!!'

I saw my first white-tailed eagle not long after that. Even though it was a distance away, I got such a powerful sense of how big this beautiful bird was. 'This is why I'm here!' I said to myself. 'This is where I want to live.' I remember calling my parents to tell them I was going to stay up here and that I'd found a lovely quaint cottage. The truth was that I was parked in a space at the ferry terminal next to a sign that said, 'No overnight sleeping'. But that car parking space served me well for nearly a year in the end. I had white-tailed eagles and otters for company. Right next to the ferry terminal were a couple of little rock pools and a small grassy mound that otters have been using as a spraint site for decades. Otters come out of the sea, nibble their catch and then want to wash their fur in freshwater. The rock pools by the terminal were a mixture of rainwater and sea water, which was good enough for them. They've got quite used to human activity and know it's not a threat. They're unmoved by the constant 'bing-bong' sounds over the Tannoy system when ferries arrive and the loud creaks and clanks you get at a ferry terminal. When I take people to these rock pools, they're always surprised that otters live here. People tend to associate otters with rivers, but if you're patient, you'll see them on our coasts. And it's a magical thing.

When I started earning a little bit from odd jobs, like chopping wood and stalking deer, I moved out of my car and rented a small caravan up the hill, overlooking the Sound of Mull. I paid £50 a month to rent the caravan. It was in a little dip that would always flood in the wintertime so I'd have to kind of 'pole-vault' inside. I'm very fond of that place, because it's where I really started seeing the otters in the lochan and the white-tailed eagles beyond. I built one of my hides on to a dry-stone wall just up the hill, to watch the eagles. This is one of the very few places in the UK where you can see both golden eagles and white-tailed eagles. Our resident golden eagle pair live round the corner and you can see two lots of white-tails from here because it's pretty much the meeting point of two different territories: Bloody Bay to the west and Ben Hiant to the east, the mountain that the sun creeps up over at dawn.

The postie delivered letters to me there at the caravan. Only I didn't really have an official address so friends and employers never knew what to write on the front of envelopes. I remember when one letter arrived addressed to: Hamza Yassin (The big guy in the caravan up the hill and left a bit), Kilchoan, Ardnamurchan, Scotland. And that's very much in keeping with the humour up here. Right next to where I used to live in the caravan, there's a cottage with the only blue plaque in the village. I know – pretty special, right? It reads: 'Nothing of Note Has Happened Here'.

I know every house up in the village and each one has a memory or a story attached. Like Jimmy Archer's place. Jimmy was a character. He had an old motorbike that he'd just ride around the village running errands. The only trouble was, the brakes hadn't worked since about 1975, so he'd stop the motorbike by scraping his wellies against the road. Which meant he needed a new pair pretty much every month. No one wanted to see what would happen when the wellies wore through, so we'd take it in turns to buy him a new pair of wellies and leave them outside his door. Just down the lane is where Jeff and Sandra live (and Peanut the pine marten). It's a badge of honour when our resident pine marten decides that she likes the look of your place!

Heading back towards the water, I drive past a woodshed with a sign up that reads: 'Chop your own wood and it'll warm you twice'. And that makes me smile because when I was in my caravan here in the winter, with no heating, chopping wood for people was the ideal job. Not only do you get a few quid in your pocket – you're also toasty warm for your troubles! Most people assume that now I'm on the telly, my wood-chopping days are behind me, but that's not how we are up here. I'm a solid odd-jobs man. I pick up prescriptions for my friends, neighbours and the wider community because I'm young, I'm in the van a lot for work and so I'll be passing the nearest chemist, which is a good 45 minutes away. If someone needs to get a washing machine off a van and into their house, they call me. If someone's found an injured animal and doesn't know what to do, they call me. Or if their camera's stopped working! Or if they're trying to learn ballroom dancing! It's a small village and we want to help each other out with whatever skills we each possess. That's the very heart of community to me. If there's anything I can do, I will do it.

And, like the tides of the Sound of Mull lapping at the shore before me, it runs both ways. If I need some wood to build a hide, or some help carrying my equipment, someone will step in to help. Or if I'm in the Small Isles filming for weeks and have gone completely crazy and need rescuing, I know Chris will be there in his RIB! As soon as I'm off the car ferry and on the Ardnamurchan peninsula, I'm not so much 'the guy on telly'. I'm more the big dude who's good at lifting things and flying drones about. I'm still occasionally introduced like this up here: 'This is my friend Hamza. He's very good at chopping wood and fixing animals. He's also on the telly.'

We get a couple of injured animals a year here. This year, we had a badger with a big wound on its flank. He was found feeding on the food left out for the pine marten living at Liz's place. Once we realized that, we waited until Peanut the pine marten wasn't around, and then added antibiotics to her food, to treat the injured badger. A week later, the wound was healing nicely. Two weeks later, the wounds were practically gone. Soon after that, the badger stopped coming for the pine marten's food because it didn't need to. It was fit and healthy enough to go and hunt again.

Like me, Ricky loves animals and steps up to help injured creatures, such as Dubhaidh, the beautiful raven from Ben Hiant that he'd been lovingly tending. Ravens really are remarkable birds, among the most intelligent of not just birds but all animals. Sadly, despite Ricky's painstaking efforts, the vet couldn't save Dubhaidh. The injuries to his feet and wings were just too severe. You do your best to save animals in need, but sometimes they're too far gone. That doesn't make it any easier, especially when you've been nursing them in your house for days or weeks. I know only too well that sadness and sense of frustration that maybe you could have done more and it was etched into Ricky's face when he walked wearily through the door of Puffin, our beloved local café, the next day. It's moving to see someone with such a profound connection with the natural world. But you can find comfort in the arms of those around you who understand what you're going through. There's a natural ebb and flow mentality here of give and take that mirrors the tides. And you value it in a different way once it brings you back to life. A few hours later, I received a message from Ricky. He'd written a poem in honour of Dubhaidh.

The prince of birds
High-flying acrobat of the air
Owning the space he lives in

Calling to family

Gathering to display and show those aeronautical
  talents

As black it seems as hell itself

Until sunlight hits the shimmering feathers

Then blues and a rainbow of oil slick brightness
  gleams back across the sky

Our friend the raven calling to show its presence

Calling to say hello

Calling to tell us I'm still here

I still live

I still fly

Dubhaidh

★ ★ ★

I came to Ardnamurchan for the wildlife, but I've stayed
for the people. I didn't know that I'd find a community
here that would embrace me as warmly as they have. I also
didn't know that I needed it. That realization dawned on
me when I started on *Strictly Come Dancing*. It was the first
time I'd stayed in London. It's funny – just before *Strictly*
started, I was camping in the Canadian Arctic with the
very real danger of a polar bear attack. That didn't worry

me. But London did. The way I approached it was to figure this would be a one- or two-week-long adventure. But as each week went by, I was still somehow in the running, which was incredible, but I found myself gazing out of the window in my hotel in Wembley dreaming of greenery. I got a bit of that with the unexpected delight of a group of ring-necked parakeets screeching past my roof, but I needed my home in the Highlands. I needed the people there. On *Strictly*, I was a small-town dude suddenly thrust under a spotlight. I was forced to learn a lot about myself – that's the truly difficult bit. Everyone thinks they know themselves, but you don't really until you've been pushed to your limits, physically, mentally and emotionally. I was completely out of my comfort zone the whole time. A fish out of water. At that time, the messages of support and calls from my friends and neighbours were the things that kept me going, like my Scottish mother, Amanda, phoning me up and saying, 'Double H, Hamza: be happy and be humble.' And I'll never forget that. You need the village to survive. When I got back to Ardnamurchan after the *Strictly* adventure, a friend asked me if I'd be going on holiday.

'I am on holiday!' I said.

Epilogue

———

I have a childlike sense of wonder that governs everything I do. I'm at my happiest when I'm outside, because you never know what's going to appear or fly over you. As my friend George McGavin told me recently: 'Observation of the natural world is something that anybody can do. An inquiring eight-year-old with a hand lens in their garden or in a woodland could see something that no one's ever seen before.'

I felt fulfilled today because I showed my friend a gannet gliding over the water at the base of the Ardnamurchan Lighthouse. He'd never seen a gannet in the wild. Whenever a friend comes to visit me here, I want to show them as many animals, trees and landscapes as I can.

And if they've brought their children, I'll sprinkle a little magic, the way it was sprinkled for me hearing the tale of the Glencoe Giant. That's the kind of thing that sets a kid's mind alight. And once it's ablaze, it'll burn forever. Nature + imagination = lifelong inspiration.

I think some people make the assumption that if you live in a remote place, you're a remote sort of person, but that's not what I've found. There's a like-minded community of wildlife lovers of all ages and all backgrounds here in Ardnamurchan. Children of Mother Nature. I love that rewilding is already happening here and that my friends and neighbours are excited about it.

In 20 years' time, I think Ardnamurchan will look quite different. I hope that we'll follow the same idea as they did around Loch Mudle, putting up deer fences and cattle grids to allow the landscape to regenerate. Out the back of my house there will be a beautiful wildflower meadow full of butterflies. I'll even hook a sound system up playing corncrake calls to invite them to nest here. Beyond my house, if I can buy the land up the hill, I'll plant sessile oaks and silver birches. And who knows, maybe my children's children will hear the sound of willow warblers from their back garden.

'A society grows great when old men plant trees the shade of which they know that they will never sit in.'

This is my version.

Thanks

———

Thanks as ever go to my wonderful parents and my Scottish family up in Ardnamurchan.

In this book, I've been fortunate enough to be able to call upon some extraordinary friends, who have contributed their time and wisdom to make this book such a special and personal project to me. To Niki Clear, Martin Mitchell, Erica McAlister, Nigel Brown, Kim Wallis, Nigel Hand, Shaila Rao, Siobhán Moran, Jack Ward, Patrick Barker and George McGavin – it was a privilege to hear your knowledge and passion and I'm in awe of all of you.

A special thank you goes to my neighbour Ricky Clark for his beautiful words.

To my agents at DML: Lou Leftwich, Jan Croxson, Borra Garson and Megan Page, thank you all.

Many thanks to my editor Jess Minocha and everyone at Octopus who has made this book as lovely as it is.

And lastly to my writer and friend Nathan Joyce. Here's to the next adventure together!

Index

About the Author

———

Hamza Yassin is a Scottish wildlife cameraman and presenter, a skilled ornithologist and the winner of the 2022 season of *Strictly Come Dancing*. Born in Sudan, Hamza moved to the UK when he was young. He has a degree in Zoology with Conservation from Bangor University and a Masters in Biological Photography and Imaging from the University of Nottingham. He made his first television appearance on the CBeebies show *Let's Go for a Walk*, in the role of Ranger Hamza. Since then, Hamza has appeared on *The One Show* and *Countryfile*, and he is a presenter on the long-running BBC series *Animal Park*. Hamza has also presented his own documentaries for the BBC (*Hamza: Strictly Birds of Prey*) and Channel

4 (*Scotland: My Life in the Wild* and *Scotland: Escape to the Wilderness*). His latest BBC documentary, *Hamza's Hidden Wild Isles*, is broadcast in 2025.

🄾 hamzayassin90
𝕏 hamzayassin3

Hamza Yassin

Be a Birder

My Love of Birdwatching and How to Get Started

'Brings a little bit of joy to us all'
Guardian

'He is delight and joy personified'
Marian Keyes

Also published by Gaia
ISBN: 9781856755108

RAISING READERS
Books Build Bright Futures

Dear Reader,

We'd love your attention for one more page to tell you about the crisis in children's reading, and what we can all do.

Studies have shown that reading for fun is the single biggest predictor of a child's future life chances – more than family circumstance, parents' educational background or income. It improves academic results, mental health, wealth, communication skills, ambition and happiness.[1]

The number of children reading for fun is in rapid decline. Young people have a lot of competition for their time. In 2024, 1 in 10 children and young people in the UK aged 5 to 18 did not own a single book at home.[2]

Hachette works extensively with schools, libraries and literacy charities, but here are some ways we can all raise more readers:

- Reading to children for just 10 minutes a day makes a difference
- Don't give up if children aren't regular readers – there will be books for them!
- Visit bookshops and libraries to get recommendations
- Encourage them to listen to audiobooks
- Support school libraries
- Give books as gifts

There's a lot more information about how to encourage children to read on our website: www.RaisingReaders.co.uk

Thank you for reading.

---

[1] OECD. 2021. 21st-century readers: developing literacy skills in a digital world. Paris, France: OECD Publishing. https://www.oecd.org/en/publications/21st-century-readers_a83d84cb-en.html

[2] National Literacy Trust, Book Ownership in 2024, November 2024 https://nlt.cdn.ngo/media/documents/Book_ownership_in_2024